→INTRODUCING

PLATO

DAVE ROBINSON & JUDY GROVES

Published in the UK in 2010
by Icon Books Ltd.,
Omnibus Business Centre,
39-41 North Road, London N7 9DP
email: info@iconbooks.co.uk
www.introducingbooks.com

Sold in the UK, Europe, South Africa
and Asia by Faber and Faber Ltd.,
Bloomsbury House,
74-77 Great Russell Street,
London WC1B 3DA
or their agents

Distributed in the UK, Europe, South
Africa and Asia by TBS Ltd.,
TBS Distribution Centre,
Colchester Road, Frating Green,
Colchester CO7 7DW

This edition published in Australia
in 2010 by Allen & Unwin Pty. Ltd.,
PO Box 8500, 83 Alexander Street,
Crows Nest, NSW 2065

Previously published in the UK
and Australia in 2000 and 2005

Reprinted 2001, 2002,
2003, 2004, 2005, 2006

This edition published in the USA
in 2010 by Totem Books
Inquiries to: Icon Books Ltd.,
Omnibus Business Centre,
39-41 North Road,
London N7 9DP, UK

Distributed to the trade in the USA
by Consortium Book Sales & Distribu
The Keg House
34 Thirteenth Avenue NE, Suite 101
Minneapolis, Minnesota 55413-1007

Distributed in Canada by
Penguin Books Canada,
90 Eglinton Avenue East, Suite 700,
Toronto, Ontario M4P 2Y3

ISBN: 978-184831-177-0

Originating editor: Richard Appignanesi

Printed by Gutenberg Press, Malta

The King of Philosophers

Plato was probably the greatest philosopher of all time, and the first to collect all sorts of different ideas and arguments into books that everyone can read. He wanted to know about everything and constantly pestered his friends and fellow philosophers for answers to his disturbing questions. He also had resolute ideas of his own, some of which seem sensible enough, and some of which now seem extremely odd. But, from the start, he knew that "doing philosophy" was a very special activity...

The World of Athens

Plato was born in 427 B.C.E. into an aristocratic family, and lived in Athens for most of his life. The 5th century city-state of Athens was probably the most civilized place in the world – a home to astronomers, biologists, logicians, artists, mathematicians, and all sorts of thinkers then loosely categorized as "lovers of wisdom" or "philosophers".

THE ATHENIAN EMPIRE EXTENDED THROUGHOUT THE MEDITERRANEAN.

AND IT WAS MAINTAINED WITH RUTHLESS EFFICIENCY.

All of the dull hard physical work was performed by slaves, so most Athenians had plenty of leisure time in which to think and talk about ideas.

BUT THEY AVOIDED THINKING TOO HARD ABOUT THE ETHICAL ISSUE OF SLAVERY ITSELF.

WOMEN DIDN'T HAVE MUCH SAY IN THE INTELLECTUAL OR PUBLIC LIFE OF THE STATE.

The actual city of Athens was small enough for everyone to know everyone else, which means that Plato's philosophy was probably directed at a specific élite audience of intellectual friends and acquaintances.

5

The Decline of Athens

Plato lived through a turbulent and finally disastrous period of Athenian history. In the Golden Age of Athens, the great statesman **Pericles** (c. 495-429 B.C.E.) had been able to unite nearly all of the other Greek city-states into a temporary alliance against the Persians, who were always threatening to invade. The union was short-lived.

It is extremely likely that Plato fought in this last war as a cavalryman. It would have been very odd for a citizen like him not to have done so. Like other young upper-class Athenians, he was probably rather ambivalent about the war.

WE ADMIRED SPARTA AS AN ARISTOCRATIC SOCIETY THAT WAS EFFICIENT AND STABLE BECAUSE IT STOOD NO NONSENSE FROM THE LOWER ORDERS.

After the war, Sparta imposed a puppet government on Athens. Plato would probably have become a part of it, like his relatives Critias and Charmides, if history had been slightly different.

7

Socrates

Plato met a charismatic philosopher called **Socrates** (470-399 B.C.E.) who completely changed his life. Socrates was a popular guru for many young Athenians, even though his appearance, personal habits and philosophical views were mocked and lampooned in the Athenian theatres and in public life. Socrates maintained that philosophy couldn't be taught, because it was really an attitude of mind rather than a body of knowledge. And like all gurus, he usually spoke in riddles and paradoxes.

THE WISE MAN IS THE ONE WHO KNOWS THAT HE IS IGNORANT.

SOCRATES INSISTS THAT PHILOSOPHERS HAVE TO QUESTION CONVENTIONAL WISDOM AND CHALLENGE TRADITIONAL BELIEFS.

YOUNG PEOPLE MUST THINK FOR THEMSELVES AND TAKE NOTHING FOR GRANTED.

Socrates was encouraging the sort of rebellious behaviour that governments and authorities usually hate. The citizens of Athens eventually threw out the puppet government of the "Thirty Tyrants", restored a democratic government, and in 399 B.C.E. had Socrates executed by forcing him to drink poison. The rather unconvincing charges against him were that he was blasphemous and that he was corrupting young people. In fact, he was probably condemned because of his continuing close friendship with two ex-pupils – Critias ("The Tyrant") and Alcibiades ("The Spartan Traitor"). Socrates, like his pupil, Plato, seems to have made disastrous choices when it came to friends.

Foreign Travels

Socrates' execution was a highly traumatic event for many young Athenians, including Plato, who left the city disgusted with all Athenian politics and politicians. At the time, he said that …

UNTIL KINGS BECOME PHILOSOPHERS OR PHILOSOPHERS, KINGS, THINGS WILL NEVER GO WELL IN THIS WORLD.

He travelled around the Mediterranean, **may** have visited Egypt, **may** have been kidnapped and ransomed by pirates, and almost certainly **did** visit some Greek colonies in Southern Italy, before he finally settled briefly in Sicily at the court of King Dionysius I. Here he met an attractive young man called Dion, who made a big impression on the middle-aged Athenian refugee. He also met the philosopher Archytas of Tarentum, who encouraged his interest in Pythagorean mathematics.

The Academy

The homesick Plato eventually returned to Athens where, circa 387 B.C.E., he established the first ever European university – called "The Academy" – in the western suburbs. In this educational institution, full-time scholars ate around the same table, argued about everything that was known, and kept the spirit of Socratic debate alive. Plato gave lectures to students on mathematics, astronomy and his theory of "Forms" whilst walking around his garden. He had a small library and perhaps even a mechanical model of the planetary orbits. Like the Pythagorean scholars of southern Italy, the members of the Academy believed that a study of mathematics held the key to all understanding.

The purpose of the Academy could sometimes confuse less studious Athenians. On one occasion, many citizens responded enthusiastically to an advertised public talk on "The Good Life", expecting to hear about happiness and self-improvement, but found that they had to sit through an obscure and interminable lecture on higher mathematics.

The Ill-Advised Visits to Syracuse

When he was 60, Plato made another disastrous visit to Syracuse in Sicily at the request of his friend Dion. Plato was supposedly employed as tutor to the young King Dionysius II, but found himself in the middle of an appalling political hornets' nest. Dion himself had been banished for plotting against the throne.

As a result, Plato seems to have experienced some "difficulty" in leaving Syracuse when he wanted to return home. By now, the beleaguered king had sensibly decided that he had more pressing things to attend to than tutorials in metaphysics.

Plato, very unwisely, returned to Syracuse when he heard that Dionysius had promised to un-banish Dion. But Dion remained banished, all of his property was confiscated and Plato would have remained in Syracuse under permanent house-arrest had not a neighbouring ruler intervened on his behalf. In 357 B.C.E., Dion invaded Syracuse and overthrew Dionysius …

BUT HE WAS THEN ASSASSINATED BY CALLIPPUS, ANOTHER OLD ACQUAINTANCE OF MINE.

This complicated story of personal betrayal, blackmail, threats and very real violence would seem to indicate that Plato was a rather poor judge of character and political circumstances. He was clearly right to give up public life for good after this last visit and remain cynical about all politicians thereafter.

The Peaceful Academic

Plato finally returned to Athens, where he taught and argued in the Academy until his death in 347 B.C.E. The Academy's most impressive student was a Macedonian from the north called **Aristotle** (384-322 B.C.E.).

I STUDIED WITH PLATO FOR 20 YEARS, BECAME HEAD OF THE ACADEMY AFTER HIS DEATH, BUT LATER FOUNDED MY OWN SCHOOL, THE LYCEUM, IN 335 B.C.E.

The Academy itself continued for many centuries until it was eventually closed down in A.D. 529 by the Christian emperor Justinian. When Plato died, he was a few years over 80 and, like most individuals who have subsequently taken up the profession of philosophy, had very little in the way of money or possessions.

Greek Civilization

The civilization of 5th-century Athens was very special, primarily because it laid the foundations of our own modern Western beliefs and values. But although the Athenians were like us in many respects, in other ways they were quite different. They admired warrior virtues, and they were probably less individualistic and more "tribal" than we are now. Because their social and cultural world was very different to ours, this means that many Greek words are difficult to translate into clear modern English equivalents.

Greek Thought

The Greeks also had a **teleological** view of the world and themselves. This means that everything in the world aimed towards an ultimate purpose or design – a good knife had to be sharp, a horse strong and obedient, a government just and efficient, and so on. So a "good" human being was one who fulfilled his function, mostly by being a good citizen. Slaves were unfortunate – they were slaves because of their "natures".

Greek religious beliefs were also very different. The Greek gods were a quarrelsome, promiscuous and often immoral bunch whom you were wise to compliment and make sacrifices to. Intelligent Greek citizens looked beyond official religion for their political and ethical values.

BY ASKING FUNDAMENTAL QUESTIONS OUTSIDE OF MYTHS, WE STARTED "DOING PHILOSOPHY".

WE QUESTIONED EVERYTHING …

MATHEMATICS, MORALITY, BIOLOGY, POLITICS, SOCIOLOGY, HISTORY, ASTRONOMY, ECONOMICS …

"Knowledge" was getting started, which means that Athenians didn't draw the rigid distinctions that we now do between different disciplines. They were the first society to refuse to take traditional answers for granted. Their attitude of mind was critical and investigative, and it is that, more than anything else, that still makes them truly "modern".

The City-States of Greece

The city-states of Greece were all well-established by the time Plato was born. They were quite unique in the ancient world. Egypt and Persia were huge, rich, monolithic and theocratic societies, whereas the Greeks lived in small, independent states which were mostly poor.

THERE ARE MANY CITY-STATES.

ALL ARE INDEPENDENT OF EACH OTHER ...

... AND GOVERNED BY VERY DIFFERENT POLITICAL SYSTEMS.

Athens was special in its frequent choice of a very direct form of democratic government which included all adult male citizens. Being an Athenian gave you privileges, but also many arduous political and public duties, like military and jury service, and if you were better off, payments for the rituals and seasonal theatre events. Athens was famous for its great dramatists, Aeschylus, Sophocles, Euripedes, Aristophanes and others.

Plato's Warnings

Plato kept warning his fellow Athenians about the immediate dangers to the city-state. Athens was threatened by external enemies: both the Persian empire and the militaristic city-state of Sparta. Athenian citizens themselves seemed perpetually quarrelsome and devoted to democratic governments which were invariably corrupt and inefficient. The intelligent young men, the citizens of the future, were being corrupted by "Sophists".

SOPHISTS TEACH THAT MORALITY IS A MATTER OF PERSONAL CHOICE AND THAT HUMAN SELFISHNESS IS ONLY "NATURAL".

Plato's *Republic* was a desperate attempt to prove how false and dangerous these ideas are. For Plato, change and progress are always associated with corruption and decay. His philosophy aimed to provide the sort of permanent moral values and durable political stability that would save Athens. What he didn't know, of course, was that the real threat lay to the north. Athens was finally "absorbed" into the Macedonian empire of **Philip the Great** (382-336 B.C.E.) and his successor, Aristotle's pupil, **Alexander the Great** (356-323 B.C.E.).

Influences on Plato: the Pre-Socratics

The three philosophers who most influenced Plato were Pythagoras, Heraclitus and Socrates. **Pythagoras** (c. 571-496 B.C.E.), born on the isle of Samos, was persecuted by the dictator Polycrates and went to live in Croton, in Greek southern Italy. Like many "pre-Socratic" philosophers of the 6th century B.C.E., he believed that there must be one underlying unity or element that constituted "everything". The pre-Socratics variously suggested that this "unity" could be water, air, fire, or atoms.

BUT I CLAIM THAT **ALL THINGS ARE NUMBERS**.

EVERYTHING THAT YOU CAN SEE AROUND YOU IS **MATHEMATICS**.

His view seems absurdly counter-intuitive. It is hard to see how clouds, trees and waves can be "mathematics". Pythagoras came to this view by discovering that the individual notes and structures of music can be explained as ratios. For him, this implied that all natural phenomena were similarly mathematical.

The Religion of Mathematics

What Pythagoras also realized was that mathematics is independent of the observable, empirical world. You can't **see** "triangularity" or the actual number "47". Mathematics is "pure" and uncontaminated. The study of it enables you to escape from the grubby inconsistencies of the physical world.

NUMBERS ARE UNIVERSAL, INCORRUPTIBLE AND ETERNALLY TRUE, AND THEIR TRUTH CAN ONLY BE REVEALED THROUGH REASON.

PYTHAGORAS DEVELOPED A PROFOUND RELIGIOUS AWE FOR NUMBERS, AND A DELIGHT IN THEIR GEOMETRIC PATTERNS.

Pythagoras founded a colony of religious mathematicians in Croton, which he ruled with iron discipline. He also believed in the existence of the immortal soul and in reincarnation. So Pythagoras was primarily responsible for establishing the widely-held Greek belief that real knowledge had to be like mathematics – universal, permanent, obtained by pure thought and uncontaminated by the senses. He also demonstrated that it was possible to found a community that could be success-fully governed by philosophers.

19

Heraclitus: Everything Changes

Heraclitus (c. 535-475 B.C.E.) had a strangely accelerated view of the world. For him, it was in a state of constant movement and change. Nothing had any permanence or reliability. His famous remark is **panta rei** – everything changes.

EVEN MOUNTAINS ARE LIKE WATERFALLS IN VERY SLOW MOTION.

THIS MEANS THAT ALL OUR BELIEFS ABOUT THE EMPIRICAL WORLD ARE ALWAYS TEMPORARY, UNRELIABLE AND CAN NEVER REALLY COUNT AS "KNOWLEDGE".

The dog we confidently claim to see in front of us was once a puppy and soon will be a corpse.

Not only is the world just "process", but everyone also sees it differently. All our beliefs about it are "observer-relative". A weight is heavy for an ordinary man but light for a weightlifter.

HELEN OF TROY WAS BEAUTIFUL TO PARIS, BUT PLAIN TO ANYONE WHO HAS SEEN THE GODDESS APHRODITE.

THERE ARE NO STABLE MEANINGS TO THE SUBJECTIVE TERMS WE USE TO DESCRIBE THE PHYSICAL WORLD. THEY ALWAYS NEED QUALIFICATION.

"This building is big" means merely – "big to me". Heraclitan scepticism about empirical knowledge reinforces the Pythagorean view. Real knowledge can be pure and permanent only if it is obtained by the mind and not through the senses.

Pure and Applied Science

After Pythagoras and Heraclitus, most Greek philosophers believed that knowledge could only come from thought, and that although observation was useful, it was an inferior and misleading way of understanding the world and the place of human beings within it.

SUCH A VIEW HELPS TO EXPLAIN WHY IT IS THAT THE ANCIENT GREEKS INVENTED EXTREMELY SOPHISTICATED MATHEMATICS, ASTRONOMY AND PHILOSOPHY ...

BUT LITTLE IN THE WAY OF **TECHNOLOGY**.

Having a large slave population to do all the hard work was also a disincentive. Why invent windmills when 20 slaves can turn a grindstone?

Socrates' View of Knowledge

But it was Socrates who inspired Plato more than any other philosopher. He was ugly, short, untidy and occasionally drunk, but immensely influential. We only know the sorts of things that Socrates said because Plato recorded them.

> THE JOB OF THE PHILOSOPHER IS TO CONCENTRATE ON HUMAN BEINGS - HOW THEY SHOULD LIVE THEIR LIVES - NOT PERFORM CEREBRAL INVESTIGATIONS INTO THE UNDERLYING STRUCTURE OF THE NATURAL WORLD.

> SOCRATES WAS OBSESSED BY THE QUESTION OF HUMAN "VIRTUE". WHAT IS IT THAT HUMAN BEINGS SHOULD STRIVE FOR?

Some philosophers had already suggested that personal pleasure and happiness were enough, but Socrates insisted that the answer was **knowledge.** The teleological purpose of human beings is to question everything and join in debate with others, in order to get as close as possible to the truth.

Socratic Dialogue

Philosophy is an odd activity. It has no obvious procedural methodologies like geometry or physics. Socrates had to invent the sorts of things that philosophy had to do, and give it a method of inquiry. He encouraged the idea that it should be a process of argument and debate. This tends to have a negative function. Participants in "Socratic dialogue" nearly always find that their answers to philosophical questions are inadequate and unacceptable.

THEY BEGIN BY THINKING THEY HAVE A GRASP OF CERTAIN CONCEPTS, BUT SOON FIND THAT THEY DON'T.

SOCRATIC DIALOGUE IS THEREFORE OFTEN BETTER AT REVEALING IGNORANCE THAN PRODUCING ANSWERS.

Philosophy's job is to clarify the sorts of questions that are being asked, and then determine what sorts of answers are acceptable. It is more a process of clarification than of discovery. Socrates' habit of pulling the rug from under complacent people's feet could obviously be very irritating, which is why his nickname was "The Gadfly". His other more complimentary nickname was "The Midwife", because he assisted with the birth of knowledge in various people.

Virtue is Knowledge

In spite of his caution, Socrates wasn't a sceptic. He did believe it was possible to have a limited knowledge about what made human beings fulfilled, and he had some firm theories about how they should live. With education, human beings could come to know their true selves, know what was good and act accordingly. This is reflected in Socrates' famous saying.

THE UNEXAMINED LIFE IS NOT WORTH LIVING.

FOR SOCRATES, THERE WAS MUCH MORE TO MORALITY THAN COLLECTIVE LEGISLATION.

Goodness was a kind of knowledge somehow encoded into the structure of the universe itself – there were natural **moral facts.** Once these were known, it would be impossible for anyone to do bad things. This means that a wicked man is merely one who is ignorant.

Claiming that morality is a kind of knowledge like any other now seems rather odd. We are no longer confident about the existence of any certain moral "facts".

Seek the Essences

Socrates also thought that every thing and every idea had a mysterious inner "essential nature" which could be revealed through the dialectic of debate. Real knowledge lay in finding out conclusive definitions. This usually involved examining many different examples of a certain concept in order to find out some common characteristic. When you've done that, you should be able to move to a general definition.

I ASK EVERYONE, "WHAT IS JUSTICE?" A CORRECT ANSWER WILL BE FOUND THAT HAS PRACTICAL APPLICATIONS.

This "essentialist" doctrine seems to work well in mathematics and geometry. The "essence" of a triangle is "a three-sided figure". But the "essential nature" of human beings, or of "Goodness", is less clear. It's because his quest was so rarely successful that Socrates suggested ignorance rather than knowledge as the normal state of the human mind.

Plato's Socrates

Plato's first philosophical works are his tribute to Socrates and his attempt to keep the tradition of Socratic debate alive. He wanted to set the record straight and tell everyone what Socrates had said. Plato uses Socrates as his spokesman in nearly all of his books. So it isn't always clear *whose* ideas are being presented at any one time. This seems not to have worried Plato much, because he saw himself as continuing a philosophical tradition. However, most scholars now think that the early dialogues are a reasonably accurate account of Socrates' views, and that the middle and later works are mostly Plato's own.

Plato and Socrates in a frontispiece to a 13th-century English fortune-telling book.

Jacques Derrida in *The Postcard* (1980) puzzles over this intriguing image of Socrates who seems to **write** what Plato **dictates** – which poses the enigma of the "written speaker".

The Euthyphro

The Euthyphro is a dialogue between Euthyphro and Socrates as they stand outside the Athens courthouse. Socrates is about to be tried and condemned to death, and yet still finds the time to discuss the crucial distinction between a morality based on religious belief and one based on philosophical reasoning. Socrates shows that it is almost impossible to derive a consistent moral code from the gods. They continually quarrel and it is never possible to please all of them all of the time. Most importantly, though, Plato (or is it Socrates?) gets Euthyphro to admit a crucial difference.

"DOING THE RIGHT THING" IS DIFFERENT TO "DOING WHAT THE GODS APPROVE".

AH, UHM ... YES, IT IS.

What is morally right is not necessarily always pious ... religion is loveable because it is loved, and morality is loved because it is loveable.

As is usually the case, Socrates pushes Euthyphro into a verbal and conceptual maze from which he cannot escape. Worried by all this rather irregular talk from a notorious blasphemer, Euthyphro is very reluctant to arrive at any unorthodox conclusions, and so makes his excuses. Socrates' views, after all, are the very ones he is about to be tried for.

SO TELL ME YOUR CONCLUSION, MY MOST WORTHY EUTHYPHRO, AND DON'T CONCEAL IT.

ANOTHER TIME, THEN, SOCRATES; AT THE MOMENT I HAVE AN URGENT ENGAGEMENT SOMEWHERE AND IT'S TIME FOR ME TO BE OFF.

True moral knowledge can only be reached through philosophical thinking and debate. It's all too easy for Euthyphro to obey religious edicts and then be confident that he has behaved morally. Morality and religion are often at odds. People can do wicked things for religious reasons, and sometimes a moral act may have to be religiously unorthodox. Only when people turn away from the dogmatism and irrationality of religion can true moral philosophy begin.

The Apology

The Apology is ostensibly an account of the series of speeches that Socrates made at his trial, before and after the sentence of death was passed. He is not at all apologetic or conciliatory, but boldly defiant. He lectures the court on the nature of philosophical debate. He claims that it is sometimes necessary to put forward ideas in which one doesn't believe in order to stimulate argument. He reluctantly admits that some of the irresponsible aristocratic young men who followed him about may have pestered their elders and betters with tedious questions. But he is firmly convinced that it is always his duty to philosophize and tell the truth as he sees it.

YOU ARE MISTAKEN IF YOU THINK THAT A MAN WHO IS WORTH ANYTHING OUGHT TO SPEND HIS TIME WEIGHING UP THE PROSPECTS OF LIFE AND DEATH.

HE HAS ONLY ONE THING TO CONSIDER IN PERFORMING ANY ACTION AND THAT IS WHETHER HE IS ACTING RIGHTLY OR WRONGLY, LIKE A GOOD MAN OR A BAD ONE.

Subsequent philosophers have warmed to these splendid declarations of intellectual independence and moral probity which mark all philosophers as heroes. Others, like the American journalist **I.F. Stone** (b. 1908), find the speech full of inconsistencies and disingenuous evasions. Socrates claimed he was actually apolitical because his own "inner voice" had told him to avoid public life. He was wise enough to realize that the life expectancy of many Athenian politicians wasn't that great. "*Anyone who intends to survive for even a short time must confine himself to private life and leave politics alone*".

31

Socrates probably **was** indirectly involved in some dangerous Athenian politics. Nevertheless, there is no doubt that he accepts his sentence with an impressive stoical calm. He ends by saying that his death will be either complete annihilation or a unique opportunity for him to meet up with the great Greek intellectuals of the past. Typically, he boasts that he will engage them in further debate. The talking will never stop.

The Crito

The Crito is an account of a discussion that took place in the State prison the night before Socrates' execution. Crito assures Socrates that he can arrange for him to escape.

As an Athenian citizen, he made a contract with the State which gave him rights but also imposed obligations. He will obey the legal processes of the State, however misguided. Furthermore, if he were to go into exile, this would only confirm his guilt in the eyes of his fellow citizens. *"When I leave this place it shall be as the victim not of a wrong done by the Law, but by my fellow men"*.

The Phaedo

The Phaedo is the famous account of Socrates' death. Socrates offers his grieving friends many different arguments to justify his belief in the immortality of his soul. He ironically points out that philosophers have always been an ascetic bunch, uninterested in bodily pleasures, and so "half dead" anyway. Philosophical thinking is a process of freeing the soul from the body: death is merely one further separation.

IT IS THE INTELLECT OR THE SOUL WHICH IS ABLE TO GRASP CONCEPTS AND IDEAS WITH THE GREATEST CLARITY, WHEREAS THE BODY IS ALWAYS THE CAUSE OF CONFUSION AND ERROR.

Life and death are coterminous – death comes from life, so some kind of life must emerge from death.

Everything that we seem to know from birth points to a previous existence.

IF THERE IS A PREVIOUS EXISTENCE, PERHAPS THERE IS A POSTHUMOUS ONE AS WELL.

The soul is invisible and divine, the body visible and mortal. Only the soul can grasp concepts that the senses cannot conceive of. The arguments pour out of him relentlessly.

The materialist Simmias remains unconvinced, however, and rather tactlessly says so.

WHEN THE BODY DIES, THE SOUL DOES ALSO.

BUT SOCRATES WAS UNDAUNTED ...

IF MY THEORY IS REALLY TRUE IT IS RIGHT TO BELIEVE IT. BUT IF DEATH IS EXTINCTION, I SHALL BE LESS LIKELY TO DISTRESS MY COMPANIONS BY GIVING WAY TO SELF PITY.

HEMLOCK

In the end, a State official arrives with a cup of poison that Socrates drinks in one go. Socrates' legs and body go cold. And then all the talking finally stops.

The Influence of Socrates on Plato

Plato produced other books which are yet more accounts of Socrates' debates with friends on various subjects: temperance (*The Charmides*), friendship (*The Lysis*), courage (*The Laches*) and ethics and education (*The Protagoras*). Socrates always claimed that he could never be a teacher, because he had no knowledge to impart. Nevertheless, he gave Plato a clear philosophical agenda.

HE ENCOURAGED ME TO THINK OF MORALITY AS A SPECIAL KIND OF KNOWLEDGE WHICH, ONCE ACCOMPLISHED, WOULD MAKE THE KNOWER ETHICALLY INFALLIBLE.

KNOWLEDGE CAN ONLY EMERGE FROM OBJECTIVE DEFINITIONS THAT ARE ABSOLUTE AND FUNDAMENTAL

Knowledge had to be as stable and fixed as the certainties of mathematics, kept safe from the Heraclitan world of change and from sceptical relativism. He concluded that it might be impossible to find these kinds of guaranteed definitions, or even to know when you'd got possession of them. The truth existed, but it was very difficult for human beings to achieve. Plato was determined to find a way out of this impasse by revealing a world of certainty that existed beyond the world of change and decay, which a few specialists would be able to reach.

The Sophists: Wisdom for Money

Athens was a marketplace for new ideas. A group of thinkers called the "Sophists" retailed their own brand of philosophy as a kind of self-help product. They travelled around giving lessons to sons of affluent families in return for large sums of money.

"SOPHOS" MEANS "WISDOM", BUT THE TROUBLE IS, THE SOPHISTS ARE MERELY CLEVER AT BEING WISE.

BUY YOUR WISDOM HERE

WE TEACH AMBITIOUS YOUNG MEN THE ART OF RHETORICAL PERSUASION TO ADVANCE THEIR CAREERS IN PUBLIC ASSEMBLIES.

For the Sophists, the "good man" was one able to dazzle and confound his opponents in political debate and so become influential and successful. The Sophists were especially popular amongst the newly rich Athenian families who had sons to put into the world.

Socrates and Plato were both hostile to the Sophists, partly because they were perceived as a threat to the old world order.

ONLY THE ARISTOCRACY SHOULD BE TAUGHT TO ARGUE AND DEBATE WITH SKILL.

AND FOR US, PHILOSOPHY IS THE PURSUIT OF KNOWLEDGE — A PURE AND NON-COMMERCIAL ACTIVITY UNDERTAKEN FOR THE GOOD OF THE SOUL.

One of Plato's students once had the impudence to ask Plato what philosophy was "for". He was given a coin as a "reward" for his studies and then dismissed as unsuitable.

Sophistic Relativism and Scepticism

The Greek historian **Herodotus** (c. 484-424 B.C.E.) had travelled abroad and seen that many beliefs and cultural practices were utterly different outside of Greece. "Custom alone is the guide." Laws and moralities differed from country to country. This was a bit of a shock for over-confident Athenians. But the Sophists drew their own conclusion.

IF MORAL BELIEFS ARE VARIOUS AND NOT UNIVERSAL, THEN PERHAPS ALL MORALITY IS JUST "MADE UP" OR A MATTER OF CONVENTION.

THEREFORE, PAY LIP SERVICE TO SECULAR LAW, KEEP OUT OF TROUBLE WITH THE AUTHORITIES, BUT ALWAYS LOOK AFTER YOUR OWN SELFISH INTERESTS.

So **cultural relativism** (different cultures have different ways of doing things) can lead to **ethical relativism** (the recognition that different cultures have different moral beliefs), which can itself easily slide into **ethical scepticism** (there are no absolute moral rules that are possible to prove), and fall finally into deeply worrying **ethical nihilism** (there are no moral rules, so you can do what you like).

Sophists maintained that words like "freedom", "loyalty", "justice" and "equality" were merely subjective human inventions which had only private meanings for each individual. Although Socrates had insisted that the young should take nothing for granted and question everything, he was convinced that this kind of empty cynicism and semantic relativism was wrong. The purpose of philosophy was to find the truth, not to "win" debates.

PHILOSOPHY IS A SERIOUS MORAL BUSINESS. IT HAS TO BE, BECAUSE RELIGION CAN NO LONGER BE RELIED UPON TO PROVIDE WISDOM.

THE REAL PHILOSOPHER MUST BE A DISINTERESTED SEEKER OF MORAL TRUTHS WHICH, ALTHOUGH DIFFICULT TO FIND, DO EXIST.

Plato carried on the crusade against these Sophist doctrines of moral cynicism and self-interest and the effects they were having on the young. Athens was in deep trouble if it had no centralized set of reliable moral values.

Protagoras

Some of these attacks on the Sophists are found in *The Protagoras* and *The Gorgias*. **Protagoras** (490-420 B.C.E.) was already a famous philosopher for whom both Socrates and Plato had some respect. It was Protagoras who said: *Man is the measure of all things, of those that are not that they are not.* (Translation: human beliefs are the inventions of human beings and relative to the knower, so no one can call another man wrong.)

PROTAGORAS WAS ALSO AN AGNOSTIC.

CONCERNING THE GODS, I CANNOT SAY WHETHER THEY EXIST OR NOT.

For Protagoras, all moral values were relative and the only criteria for action were things like self-preservation and expediency. But he was also a defender of democratic ideals.

POLITICAL STABILITY IS BEST PRESERVED IF EVERYONE FEELS THEY CAN HAVE A SAY IN GOVERNMENT.

SOCRATES AND I DISAGREE ABOUT THIS AS WELL.

GOVERNMENT SHOULD BE LEFT TO A GROUP OF EXPERTS.

In *The Protagoras*, everyone finally agrees that the usual quest to define "virtue", or what is best for human beings, must be abandoned, and that they must all remain ignorant. Callicles, the Sophist in *The Gorgias*, is a rather less attractive character. His view is that law and morality are merely human conventions. A clever man should put himself above the law, be strong and dominate others in his search for self-gratification.

The Meno

The Meno makes yet another attempt to provide an adequate definition of "virtue". Socrates' final conclusion is that virtue cannot be taught. It is a divine dispensation given to all, even though only a very few are ever able to "recollect" it. Meno then asks Socrates to explain something.

> WHAT DO YOU MEAN WHEN YOU SAY THAT WE DON'T LEARN ANYTHING, BUT THAT WHAT WE CALL LEARNING IS RECOLLECTION?

This time, we are probably listening to Plato's ideas rather than those of Socrates. For Plato, knowledge is something we are already born with, and so "learning" is simply forcing this knowledge to resurface into our conscious minds. Socrates neatly illustrates this by asking one of Meno's uneducated slave boys about geometry.

44

After a bit of prompting, the boy seems able to perform quite complex geometrical calculations.

From this fact, Socrates draws some rather remarkable conclusions. We know the boy didn't learn it in this life, so he must have learnt it before he was born in some kind of non-physical existence. In conclusion, he has an immortal soul, as does everybody else. Learning is therefore a process of **anamnesis**, a recollection from a pre-natal state of the soul.

Problems with Anamnesis

It would be rather nice to prove the immortality of the soul from a geometry lesson, but unfortunately there's a lot of jumping to conclusions in Plato's argument.

A KNOWLEDGE OF GEOMETRY MIGHT BE INNATE FROM BIRTH.

BUT NOT NECESSARILY BECAUSE OF TEACHING IN A PREVIOUS LIFE.

OR THE SOUL MIGHT EXIST BEFORE BIRTH BUT NOT AFTER DEATH.

The main problem is that Plato never really offers us any convincing proof that the slave boy really does possess an innate knowledge of geometry.

Socrates prompts the boy with "closed" questions (ones that require only a "yes" or "no" answer), so the boy can probably guess which is the correct answer from the inflexions in the philosopher's voice.

HE WORKS IN MENO'S HOUSE, AND SO, PRESUMABLY, ALREADY HAS SOME KNOWLEDGE OF MATHEMATICS AND SHAPES.

GO AND GET THE EIGHT ROUND PLATES AND THE SQUARE CHOPPING BOARD.

BUT THE PHILOSOPHER AND THE ARISTOCRAT ASSUME THAT THE BOY IS A MENTAL BLANK UNTIL PROMPTED.

WHICH TELLS YOU MORE ABOUT THEM THAN ABOUT ME!

The Meno began the debate about the extent of the *innate abilities* of the human mind that continues to this day amongst linguists, mathematicians, psychologists and philosophers. There is a considerable amount of evidence to suggest that the human mind is indeed specifically designed to do mathematics and learn languages. So even though Plato's methods seem flawed, his initial conclusions may well be correct.

Introduction to Plato's *Republic*

The Republic is Plato's major philosophical work – his attempt to show everyone what the ideal State would be like. It's an astonishing book, full of ideas and arguments about knowledge, religion, the soul, ethics, politics, education, feminism, war, art, and many other things besides. *The Republic* is a "closed" text which tries to provide definitive and prescriptive answers to most of the problems and questions raised by Plato's friends and contemporaries. Nearly all of the ideas are related to each other. This makes for neatness and consistency, but it means that if one central pillar of the philosophical edifice is called into question, then the whole system collapses. But, first of all, it is the context of the discussion – Athens itself – that is important.

IT IS TALK, SHEER TALK, AND THE JOY OF TALKING THAT IS THE PRIME ATTRACTION OF ATHENS.

49

Athens and the Perfect State

We know that Athens was an extraordinary place. There was nowhere else in the world where free and open discussion was tolerated so much. Athens attracted intellectuals from all over the Mediterranean, many of whom appear in this book. The city-states had been in existence for many years, and were no longer a novelty. But Greek colonies were still springing up all over the place, governed in all sorts of different ways. This means that discussion about what a "perfect" society would be like was quite a practical concern and not just an academic exercise. Most of the questions that Plato explores concern the relationship of the individual to the State, and they're all discussed in *The Republic*.

WHAT is it that binds a State together and gives it stability**?**
IS the State something "natural" and inevitable, or is it cultural and changeable**?**
ARE human beings co-operators or competitors**?**
HOW should citizens be educated**?**
WHAT is knowledge**?**
ARE human beings good or vicious**?**
ARE men equal? If so, in what sense**?**
DO they have a shared culture**?**
ARE laws necessary? Who decides what they are**?**
WHY do we have to obey laws**?**
WHAT happens if different people disagree about things**?**
DO different people have different roles in society**?**
SHOULD everyone have a say in how things are run, or should a few experts tell us all what to do**?**
DOES the State have some kind of purpose or end**?**
IS the State a good thing or a bad thing**?**

Preliminary Discussions

Plato brings philosophy to life by reproducing the interactions between all kinds of individuals with different personalities and beliefs. *The Republic* begins with everyone making an attempt to establish the definition of "right conduct" or "behaving well". Cephalus, a rich businessman, innocently suggests that a decent enough definition might be simply "to pay back your debts", which is easy for Socrates to demolish.

YOU WOULDN'T RETURN A BORROWED SWORD TO A DERANGED MADMAN, FOR EXAMPLE. THIS EXCEPTION PROVES THAT "DEBT-PAYING" CANNOT BE A GOOD DEFINITION OF "RIGHT CONDUCT".

POLEMARCHUS HAS ANOTHER SUGGESTION.

DOING GOOD TO ONE'S FRIENDS AND HARM TO ONE'S ENEMIES.

SOCRATES DISPOSES OF THIS BY SHOWING THAT IT CAN NEVER BE GOOD TO HARM SOMEONE DELIBERATELY.

As always, Socrates isn't asking for some examples of good behaviour, or an account of how people use certain moral words, but for a conclusive definition of the very "essence" of right conduct.

51

Thrasymachus

Cephalus and Polemarchus are amateurs and easily answered.
Thrasymachus is a professional Sophist philosopher from Chalcedon,
a visitor to Athens who makes his living from teaching oratory. For
Thrasymachus, all moral and political codes of behaviour are a kind of
racket, imposed by the strong onto the gullible weak. This is a further
elaboration of the views of Callicles in *The Gorgias*.

IN THE NATURAL WORLD, THE STRONG ALWAYS HAVE POWER OVER THE WEAK. THERE IS NO REASON TO EXPECT HUMAN SOCIETIES TO BE DISSIMILAR.

DIFFERENT STATES HAVE DIFFERENT LEGAL AND MORAL RULES, ACCORDING TO WHO IS IN POWER AT ANY ONE TIME.

Many contemporary Athenians would have agreed with him that "might is right". The peaceful citizens of Melos, who had wished to remain neutral in the wars between Athens and Sparta, protested at the injustice of the Athenian demand that they joined forces. They refused to fight. The Athenians weren't much interested in what was "just", and so massacred all the male citizens. Thrasymachus concludes his argument by recommending a life of self-interest.

OBEY SOCIETY'S LAWS WHEN YOU HAVE TO, BUT BREAK THEM WHEN YOU CAN GET AWAY WITH IT. BY DOING THIS YOU'LL HAVE A BETTER LIFE.

The Poor Response

Plato's arguments put by Socrates against Thrasymachus are fairly weak. A powerful government might pass laws that turned out to be against their interests, so Thrasymachus' definition of "morality" is invalid.

A DOCTOR'S SKILLS ARE PRACTISED IN THE INTERESTS OF HIS PATIENTS, SO A RULER'S WILL ALWAYS BE IN THE INTERESTS OF HIS SUBJECTS.

THE UNJUST MAN DOES NOT HAVE A BETTER LIFE, BECAUSE HUMAN BEINGS JUST AREN'T DESIGNED TO BE IMMORAL.

Injustice is divisive because even a society of crooks could not exist, if everyone followed these recommendations of selfishness.

Some Better Arguments

But any government that passed a law that went against its own interests would soon repeal it. Some wealthy doctors are less altruistic than Plato suggests. (Even if not all doctors and politicians are solely motivated by self-interest, as Thrasymachus suggests.) And it is also very difficult to know if the "purpose" of human beings is to be moral, immoral or amoral.

LIKE OTHER SOPHISTS, THRASYMACHUS BELIEVES IN THE FICTION OF "ORIGINAL" HUMAN BEINGS AS AMORAL AND PRE-SOCIAL.

HE INVENTS THIS FICTION TO SUGGEST THAT SOCIETY AND THE STATE ARE ARTIFICIAL AND UNNECESSARY LIMITATIONS ON OUR "NATURAL" SELVES.

It is both a cynical and a romantic view. But the truth could equally be that what makes human beings "human" at all is that they are, in fact, intrinsically "social" and so inevitably "moral".

The Ideological View of Morality

Thrasymachus' ideas resurface in later political philosophies. The German philosopher **Friedrich Nietzsche** (1844-1900), for example, maintained that political and moral doctrines could never be objective or disinterested.

THEY ARE ALWAYS THE BELIEFS OF ONE STRONG GROUP IMPOSED ON OTHERS.

FOR **KARL MARX** (1818-83), MORAL BELIEFS HAVE ALWAYS BEEN "IDEOLOGICAL".

THEY SEEM "NATURAL", BUT IN FACT INVARIABLY SERVE THE INTEREST OF THE DOMINANT CLASS. SO THE RICH WILL CEASELESSLY STRESS THE IMMORALITY OF THEFT.

THE SOPHIST VIEW SEEMS ALMOST CONVINCING.

But Plato may be wiser to insist that we have always been social beings, and so will always have to agree about what is acceptable or unacceptable behaviour. A moral code of some kind is inescapable. Even the poorest man in a very elementary kind of society has some property he wishes to protect. Without such agreements, human societies wouldn't get off the ground at all, even if it's true that the rich and powerful usually get the best deal out of the arrangement.

Glaucon and Adeimantus

The debate about "right conduct" is continued by two of Plato's brothers – Adeimantus and Glaucon. Glaucon is extremely cynical about human nature. Imagine you had the famous magic ring of Gyges that made you invisible on request. What would you do with it?

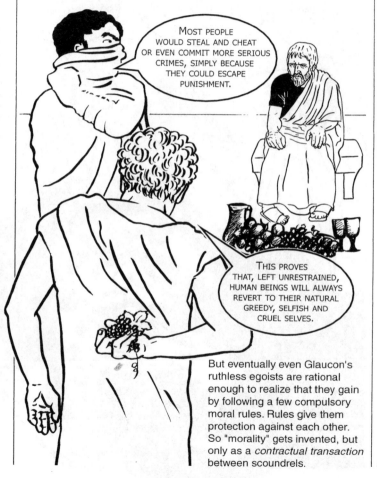

MOST PEOPLE WOULD STEAL AND CHEAT OR EVEN COMMIT MORE SERIOUS CRIMES, SIMPLY BECAUSE THEY COULD ESCAPE PUNISHMENT.

THIS PROVES THAT, LEFT UNRESTRAINED, HUMAN BEINGS WILL ALWAYS REVERT TO THEIR NATURAL GREEDY, SELFISH AND CRUEL SELVES.

But eventually even Glaucon's ruthless egoists are rational enough to realize that they gain by following a few compulsory moral rules. Rules give them protection against each other. So "morality" gets invented, but only as a *contractual transaction* between scoundrels.

Psychological Egoists

Glaucon's is a depressing view of human nature which is sometimes called "psychological egoism".

HUMAN BEINGS ARE AS FEROCIOUS AND PITILESS AS PREDATORY BEASTS. MORALITY IS THEREFORE MERELY A CONVENIENCE.

MY BROTHER ADEIMANTUS AGREES WITH THIS ANALYSIS AND SUPPORTS THE CONCLUSION OF THRASYMACHUS.

THE BEST THING IS TO "DO WRONG AND AVOID BEING FOUND OUT".

"Contract theory", then, offers a "naturalist" explanation of morality. Ethics is merely an expedient human convention.

The Social Contract Theory of Morality

This cynical view of human nature and ethics is one that has attracted several other philosophers, notably the Englishman **Thomas Hobbes** (1588-1679). He used it to explain why we need strong authoritarian governments – to **enforce** these contractually agreed moral rules.

LIFE WITHOUT GOVERNMENTS IS BARBARIC. WITHOUT THEM, PEOPLE DO INDEED BEHAVE AS IF THEY WERE "INVISIBLE" – BECAUSE THERE ARE NO SANCTIONS AGAINST WRONGDOING.

Life without governments soon becomes "nasty, brutish and short". So it's no surprise to find that people who like strong governments usually also tend to have a pessimistic view of human nature.

But Is It True?

Perhaps wisely, Plato doesn't bother to argue against these cynical views, but just proceeds with his own unique theories about human nature, society, ethics and politics. Psychological egoist explanations of all human behaviour usually tend to be self-confirming and difficult to refute.

Contractual explanations of society, morality and governments also rely on this bizarre story of solitary individuals roaming around in a pre-societal state who then meet and arrange "contracts" with each other.

Plato's Epistemology

Up to this point in *The Republic*, Plato allows a whole range of different and often subversive philosophers to have their say, many of whom now sound rather modern in their views. But then *The Republic* deteriorates into a virtual monologue in which Socrates' companions rather meekly agree with everything he says, and all this lively debate ends.

Before we continue with Plato's politics or ethics, however, it is essential to have a firm grasp on his theory of knowledge (his "epistemology"), because everything else stems from this. Plato's theory of knowledge is really what made him famous, even though no one fully understands it, and Plato himself eventually had grave reservations about it.

NEVERTHELESS, ALL OF PLATO'S PHILOSOPHICAL IDEAS ABOUT ETHICS, POLITICS, EDUCATION, ART - AND VIRTUALLY EVERYTHING ELSE - REST ON IT.

AND, AS WE'VE ALREADY SAID, IF THE EPISTEMOLOGY IS SHOWN TO BE INVALID, THEN THE REST OF HIS PHILOSOPHY ALSO COLLAPSES.

61

What is Knowledge?

There are two kinds of knowledge. One is the everyday kind of knowledge we have of the world, which we get through our senses (usually called "empirical" knowledge). Plato thought that this kind of knowledge was useful enough for ordinary people to go about their everyday lives. But it wasn't the real thing. Like Heraclitus, Pythagoras, and maybe Socrates, Plato thought that the empirical world was a kind of illusion, a veil that hid the real truth from us.

THE EVERYDAY WORLD IS FULL OF SEEMINGLY DIFFERENT THINGS WHICH ARE INHERENTLY UNSTABLE AND ALWAYS IN THE PROCESS OF CHANGE.

DIFFERENT PEOPLE EXPERIENCE THIS SURFACE WORLD IN DIFFERENT WAYS, AND HAVE DIFFERENT VIEWS ABOUT ITS QUALITIES.

ITS SIZE, WEIGHT, ATTRACTIVENESS, AND SO ON.

This means that they can only ever have "opinions" about this world, not knowledge as such. Any permanent or reliable knowledge of this sensory world is impossible. We all live surrounded by shadows, dreams, reflections and inferior copies of something better.

Universals and Particulars

The world we see around us is full of "particulars" – individual examples of things: giraffes, pencils, democracies, friends, red doors, tables. All of these things are also "contingent" – they can only exist in a specific time and place. In order to make sense of this world full of millions of different particulars, we sensibly put them into groups or classes, so that the world gets simpler and we can have a better grip on it.

IT'S NOT ALWAYS CLEAR WHETHER THESE CLASSES ARE NATURAL AND REALLY "OUT THERE", OR WHETHER THEY'RE A CONVENIENT HUMAN CLASSIFICATION SYSTEM BASED ON OUR OWN GENERALIZATIONS.

OCCASIONALLY, THINGS CROP UP THAT DON'T "FIT" INTO ANY OF THE CLASSES WE ASSUME ARE "NATURAL" – LIKE THE DUCK-BILLED PLATYPUS, AN EGG-LAYING MAMMAL.

When we look up any word in a dictionary, like "giraffe" or "pencil", we get a definition of these **universals** or classes. The dictionary provides a definition based on what all giraffes have in common. It doesn't refer us to a particular one called "Raymond" living in London Zoo.

Paradigms and Copies

The world is full of particular individual giraffes that "belong" to the universal or class called "the giraffe". Exactly what universals **are** is one of those puzzles that most people sensibly ignore, but which has always worried philosophers. Plato was the first philosopher to see that universals are problematic.

> I EXPLAIN THEM BY SAYING THAT THE INDIVIDUAL PARTICULAR GIRAFFE THAT WE SEE, LIKE RAYMOND, MUST BE AN INFERIOR COPY OF SOME PERFECT AND PERMANENT "UNIVERSAL GIRAFFE".

That's how we know what those long-necked creatures are in the first place, when we see individual examples of them. Exactly how this "perfect giraffe" exists, what kind of reality it possesses, and who can actually experience it, are questions Plato tried to give answers to, but not always very successfully. He advances a "two-world" system of epistemology – **perfect forms** and **imperfect copies**.

The Puzzling World of Forms

This world of perfect **paradigms** or blueprints is usually called Plato's world of ideal "Forms" or, more confusingly, the world of "Ideas". Plato gives different and often contradictory accounts of it, and he never seems to have worked it all out very clearly. His Forms are eternal and unchanging, the perfect patterns for the more humble particulars in our commonplace world.

FORMS EXIST SEPARATELY FROM HUMAN BEINGS AND PARTICULAR OBJECTS, AND CAN BE "RECOLLECTED" ONLY IN THE MINDS OF A FEW TALENTED AND WELL-TRAINED INDIVIDUALS.

ONCE THESE EXPERTS FIND AND KNOW THESE FORMS, THEY BECOME INFALLIBLE AUTHORITIES ABOUT EVERYTHING.

The Forms are also arranged hierarchically in some kind of structure. The Form of "The Chair" is relatively trivial and low, whereas the Form of "The Just Society" is a very important one near the top. It's an odd and puzzling epistemology, often mystical and difficult to understand or pin down. This is partly because it is conceived of as a kind of "vision", and therefore not directly communicable.

Why Plato Needed the Forms

We know how Heraclitus impressed many Greek philosophers with his vision of a continually moving and unreliable material world. One response to this philosophy is to conclude that no knowledge is possible – the view of the sceptics. Plato's solution is to suggest that there is an **alternative** world of unchangeable ideas and it is **there** that true knowledge lies.

HERACLITUS ENCOURAGED THE IDEA THAT IT IS POINTLESS LOOKING FOR KNOWLEDGE IN THE EMPIRICAL WORLD.

BUT PYTHAGORAS DEMONSTRATED THAT MATHEMATICAL KNOWLEDGE LAY BEYOND THIS MATERIAL WORLD.

You can make an inferior copy of a circle by drawing one in the sand, but "Circularity" itself is an idealized concept that only the mind can conceive of. You can buy six eggs, but you cannot ever find a "6", except in the mind.

A Short Digression

Whether all knowledge actually does have to be like maths is, of course, highly debatable. Plato never seems to have been very interested in knowledge of how things change, and seems to have confused "knowledge" with "permanence". Modern scientists do not share his contempt for empirical observation.

MATHEMATICAL EXPLANATIONS OF THE UNIVERSE ARE ACCORDED THE STATUS OF "MODELS".

UNTIL THESE MODELS ARE MEASURED AGAINST NATURE, OFTEN BY HIGHLY INGENIOUS EXPERIMENTS.

Mathematics can also point the way to newer and different kinds of empirical investigations. The two kinds of knowledge aren't different in degree, but in kind. Maths isn't "better", but "different".

Socratic Definitions

As we have seen, Socrates spent most of his life unsuccessfully trying to establish definitions by asking questions. When he asks "What is Courage?", he doesn't want a list of examples, but a definition of "Courage itself". He assumes that once he knows what Courage actually **is**, he will always know how to apply the concept to particular individuals in any set of circumstances.

PLATO SEEMS TO HAVE SHARED THIS BELIEF IN THE IMPORTANCE OF DEFINITION.

ONE WAY OF FINDING OUT HOW TO GET THIS KIND OF DEFINITION IS TO ASK WHAT IT IS THAT DIFFERENT THINGS HAVE IN COMMON.

IF YOU DO THIS, HE THOUGHT, THERE'S A GOOD CHANCE THAT YOU'LL FIND OUT THEIR "ESSENTIAL NATURE".

A good knife, a good soldier, a good dog, all have one thing in common; so, by examining these different examples carefully, it should be possible to find what "Goodness itself" actually is. You would then have a sensible working definition of the word "good", but more vitally, a deep insight into the essence of "Goodness itself".

Words, Ideas and Things

Socrates was usually very unclear about whether he was talking about words, ideas or things. (The Greek language lacked speech marks, which probably helped to confuse matters.) It's often possible to arrive at workable definitions of *words*, but there are frequently no "real definitions" of *things*.

IT'S VERY EASY TO CONVINCE ONESELF, WHEN ASKING A QUESTION LIKE "WHAT IS JUSTICE?", THAT THERE IS A REAL ANSWER.

BUT USUALLY ALL WE CAN EVER GET ARE ALTERNATIVE DEFINITIONS AND EXPLANATIONS.

IT ALSO DOESN'T HELP IF YOU ASSUME THAT BECAUSE YOU **CAN** GET THESE KINDS OF DEFINITIONS FOR MATHEMATICS AND GEOMETRY, THAT YOU CAN GET THEM FOR EVERYTHING ELSE.

Definitions and Forms

The quest for absolute definitions seems finally to have been abandoned by Socrates, although he always thought they existed somehow. He wanted to restore stability to language so that there would be some point to philosophical debate.

THERE'S NO POINT IN DISCUSSING SOMETHING IF YOU DON'T KNOW WHAT IT IS YOU ARE TALKING ABOUT.

SOCRATES WAS ALWAYS CONVINCED THAT A VERY SPECIAL KIND OF CERTAIN KNOWLEDGE WAS POSSIBLE.

HERACLITUS SAID THAT IT COULD NEVER BE OF THINGS IN THIS WORLD.

I CONCLUDE THAT IT MUST BE OF THINGS IN ANOTHER KIND OF WORLD.

And in his books, like *The Phaedo* and *The Meno*, Plato is stumbling towards the startling new doctrine which finally concluded the crusade for ultimate definitions.

We are all born with knowledge of the Forms, because we have encountered them in our earlier lives. That is why we are able to interpret all of the information provided by our senses.

... WHAT PHILOSOPHERS CALL "KNOWLEDGE BY ACQUAINTANCE".

Forms and Particulars

Plato explains how it is possible to find perfect definitions. He draws a clear distinction between all of the earthly particulars that exemplify beauty and the idea of "Beauty itself", because it is that which we want to know.

"Beauty itself" exists separately from beautiful things, which are themselves only known to us as "beautiful" because we have some vague apprehension of the "Form" of Beauty in our minds.

The Relationship between Forms and Particulars

The relationship between Forms and particulars is a puzzling one which Plato tried, but never succeeded, to explain satisfactorily. The theory evolved and changed over time, and is often inconsistent. Sometimes Plato suggests that the Forms are "shared" by individual particulars, sometimes he suggests that particulars "imitate" the Forms.

FORMS ARE MORE "REAL" THAN PARTICULARS, BECAUSE, UNLIKE PARTICULARS, THEY ARE ETERNAL AND UNCHANGING.

AUTHENTIC PHILOSOPHICAL KNOWLEDGE CAN ONLY EVER BE OF THESE "FORMS" ...

... BECAUSE FORMS ARE THE ONLY ENTITIES WHICH ARE PERMANENT AND STABLE.

Knowledge of the Forms is also only possible through the intellect in a process of discovery which Plato mysteriously compares to "seeing" with some kind of "inner eye".

Linguistic Determinism

The Greek language was lively, rich[ly] framed in such a way as to make it a[...] produce his idealist theory. Greek al[...] formulated as "**The** Beautiful" – tò k[...] thinking that "Beauty" actually "exist[...] "to know" always takes a direct obje[...] Meno, that he is rich".

THIS ENCOURAGES YOU TO THINK THAT KNOWING **SOMETHING** IS SIMILAR TO THE PROCESS [...] GETTING TO KNOW **SOMEONE** ...

Forms and Particulars

Plato explains how it is possible to find perfect definitions. He draws a clear distinction between all of the earthly particulars that exemplify beauty and the idea of "Beauty itself", because it is that which we want to know.

BUT WHERE DOES THIS STRANGE ENTITY "BEAUTY ITSELF" EXIST?

OBVIOUSLY IT MUST EXIST SEPARATELY FROM THE HUMDRUM PARTICULAR THINGS IN THIS WORLD, BECAUSE IT HAS TO BE PERFECT.

"Beauty itself" exists separately from beautiful things, which are themselves only known to us as "beautiful" because we have some vague apprehension of the "Form" of Beauty in our minds.

The Relationship between Forms and Particulars

The relationship between Forms and particulars is a puzzling one which Plato tried, but never succeeded, to explain satisfactorily. The theory evolved and changed over time, and is often inconsistent. Sometimes Plato suggests that the Forms are "shared" by individual particulars, sometimes he suggests that particulars "imitate" the Forms.

FORMS ARE MORE "REAL" THAN PARTICULARS, BECAUSE, UNLIKE PARTICULARS, THEY ARE ETERNAL AND UNCHANGING.

AUTHENTIC PHILOSOPHICAL KNOWLEDGE CAN ONLY EVER BE OF THESE "FORMS" ...

... BECAUSE FORMS ARE THE ONLY ENTITIES WHICH ARE PERMANENT AND STABLE.

Knowledge of the Forms is also only possible through the intellect in a process of discovery which Plato mysteriously compares to "seeing" with some kind of "inner eye".

We are all born with knowledge of the Forms, because we have encountered them in our earlier lives. That is why we are able to interpret all of the information provided by our senses.

WE ONLY RECOGNIZE RAYMOND AS A PARTICULAR GIRAFFE BECAUSE HE'S A COPY OF THE FORM OF "THE GIRAFFE" THAT WE ALREADY "KNOW".

THIS IS HOW PLATO'S THEORY EXPLAINS WHY THINGS ARE AS THEY ARE.

Beautiful things are beautiful because they partake in the Form of Beauty. We recognise yellow things because they all participate in the same Perfect Yellow. And so on. The more you try to explain it, the weirder it sounds. But it made a lot of sense to many 5th century Greeks, primarily because of the language they thought and spoke with.

Linguistic Determinism

The Greek language was lively, richly poetic and flexible. But it was framed in such a way as to make it almost inevitable that Plato would produce his idealist theory. Greek abstract nouns like "Beauty" were formulated as "**The** Beautiful" – **tò kalón** – which pushes you into thinking that "Beauty" actually "exists" in some way. The Greek verb "to know" always takes a direct object, so Plato would say "I know Meno, that he is rich".

THIS ENCOURAGES YOU TO THINK THAT KNOWING **SOMETHING** IS SIMILAR TO THE PROCESS OF GETTING TO KNOW **SOMEONE** ...

... WHAT PHILOSOPHERS CALL "KNOWLEDGE BY ACQUAINTANCE".

For Plato, getting knowledge is like meeting someone or something, like having a relationship. So if you know a concept like "Beauty Itself", then you've "met" it. The Greek word for "True" – **aletheia** – was the same as the word for "Real". So what is true must be real.

THE WORD FOR "WORD" – **ONOMA** – IS THE SAME AS THE WORD FOR "NAME".

SO THE WORD FOR "BEAUTY" IS ALSO ITS NAME, WHICH IMPLIES THAT IT EXISTS.

If the words that Plato thought with behaved like this, it's no great surprise that he came to believe that universals were like big, super, ghostly particulars.

It's All Greek

Not everyone would agree that ancient Greek was awkward for doing philosophy. For the German philosopher **Martin Heidegger** (1889-1976), Greek was the "original home of Being", not only the first but fundamental language that establishes all later philosophy. German, like Greek, precedes its nouns with masculine, feminine and neuter articles, which also allows Heidegger to think "oddly" of "**The** Nothingness", *Das Nichts*.

FOR ALONG WITH GERMAN, THE GREEK LANGUAGE IS THE MOST POWERFUL AND SPIRITUAL OF ALL LANGUAGES.

BESIDES, GREEK DIDN'T STOP ARISTOTLE FROM THINKING THAT PLATO'S "FORMS" WERE MISTAKEN.

LANGUAGE CAN INFLUENCE YOUR THINKING, BUT NOT WHOLLY CONTROL YOUR MIND.

LOGOS

NO LANGUAGE IS EVER FREE OF ITS OWN "BEWITCHMENTS".

Ludwig Wittgenstein (1889-1951) thought and wrote in German, like Heidegger, but with the very different purpose of combating language "traps" and "bewitchments".

78

Perfect Knowledge: Perfect Republic

Plato desperately wanted an unassailable philosophical system that would last forever against the uncertainties of the Sophists and their destructive moral and political cynicism. By inventing this "incontrovertible" epistemology, he thought he could establish firm moral and political structures for his Republic.

THOSE WHO KNOW THIS PERFECT KNOWLEDGE WILL BE THOSE WHO SHOULD RULE.

Plato always seemed to have preferred perfection to life. Like Pythagoras, he also thought that his neat explanatory patterns must be true because of their interlocking symmetry.

Neat Answers

The Forms had to be authentic because they gave such neat answers to so many different philosophical questions.

THE FORMS EXPLAIN WHAT "REAL KNOWLEDGE" IS, AS OPPOSED TO "BELIEF" (OR EMPIRICAL KNOWLEDGE), AND WHY IT CAN ONLY BE REACHED BY THE MIND.

THEY EXPLAIN WHY THINGS ARE AS THEY ARE. RED THINGS ARE RED BECAUSE (RATHER MYSTERIOUSLY) THE FORM OF "RED" CAUSES THEM TO BE THAT WAY.

THEY EXPLAIN HOW WE ARE ABLE TO APPLY GENERAL WORDS LIKE "BIG" AND "RED" TO THE WORLD.

THEY EXPLAIN WHAT IS REAL.

THEY EXPLAIN HOW WE ARE ABLE TO MAKE VALUE JUDGEMENTS OF ALL KINDS. (WE KNOW A "GOOD BED" WHEN WE SEE ONE, BECAUSE OF ITS CLOSENESS TO THE FORM OF "THE BED".)

But the Forms were rather more than a mystical consumer guide. They also provided moral and political standards which would enable a few gifted experts to save Athens from all moral and political uncertainty, and so preserve it forever.

Criticisms of the Theory of Forms

Plato himself eventually realized that there were several problems with his theory, and he voiced them in *The Parmenides*, which makes some scholars think that Plato finally abandoned his theory of Forms altogether. The problems all centre on the puzzling relationship between Forms and particulars.

This "third man argument" is an example of what philosophers call "infinite regress". It doesn't prove that the theory of Forms is wrong, but it does point to something very odd about it.

More Problems

Plato also realized that if particulars "share" a Form in some way, then presumably they all possess a **part** of the Form. This means that Forms are both "one" and "many", which is not very logical. Plato was also unsure about whether there were Forms for man-made objects.

IF THE FORMS ARE ETERNAL AND UNCHANGING, THERE WOULD HAVE TO BE FORMS FOR THINGS NOT YET INVENTED ...

... LIKE TALKING VACUUM CLEANERS AND FLYING CARS, WHICH SEEMS ODD.

And if all particulars in the world are copies of Forms, then presumably there must be Forms for nasty and unpleasant particulars, for dirt and dandruff, cholera and war. So it's not possible for the Forms always to be immaculate ideals **and** universals.

Consequences

The theory of Forms sets up dreadful confusions between things, thoughts, ideas and words. It's the **ontology** (or "reality") of the Forms that is the central problem – Plato often refers to them as if they are just rather special incorporeal particulars that exist in some unspecified place, as well as in the human mind. This leads to all sorts of odd questions.

> WHAT DOES THE FORM OF THE CHAIR LOOK LIKE?

> IS THE FORM OF "BEAUTY" ITSELF BEAUTIFUL?

Plato also claims that only the Forms are "real" and that somehow particulars are "less real", as if reality were a matter of degree. It's a weird idea, and one that **Lewis Carroll** (1832-98) had fun with in his gradually fading Cheshire Cat, which oscillates between being real, half-real and non-existent.

True and Certain Knowledge

Plato conceives of knowledge as something that only a few experts will ever possess. Because he believes that "knowing" and "meeting" are virtually the same thing, he then maintains that real knowledge has to be a kind of personal and mystical encounter.

Nowadays we would be very suspicious of this claim. We like to think of knowledge as something that **has** to be communicable, that can be stored in libraries and on CD-ROMs, made available to all and shared by different kinds of communities.

PLATO ALSO THOUGHT THAT ONCE YOU "KNEW" SOMETHING, THEN YOU'D NEVER MAKE MISTAKES.

WE ARE NOW MORE "FALLIBILIST".

We think of knowledge as something more provisional – something that might change, and we are less than absolutely certain about what we think we know.

So What Are Universals?

Plato's star pupil, Aristotle, thought that universals were "real" but didn't exist separately from individual particulars. Others, like the British Empiricist philosophers, maintained that universals are a kind of mental image that we arrive at by a process of abstraction. We see lots of trees and so generalize them into one mental image of "The Tree", which enables us to use the general term "tree" appropriately. But what a "mental tree" actually looks like became a major problem for the philosopher **John Locke** (1632-1704).

A FIR?
AN OAK?
A MAPLE?

These problems naturally arise if, like Plato, you envisage thinking as being like examining internal mental imagery.

"Nominalists" seem more sensible, because they claim that universals are merely words. This means that the only thing that trees have in common is that we ourselves apply the general term "tree" to them. But this suggests that there is no correspondence at all between the world as it is and our linguistic practice, which is a coincidence that is rather hard to accept.

PERHAPS OUR KNOWLEDGE OF UNIVERSALS IS NO MORE THAN KNOWING HOW TO USE GENERAL TERMS.

OR HOW TO RECOGNIZE "FAMILY RESEMBLANCES" BETWEEN DIFFERENT THINGS.

Wittgenstein suggested that our "craving" for definitive generalities can never be ultimately satisfied, and is rather unhealthy. But it would be wrong to think that "the problem of universals" has been explained away. Plato started a philosophical problem that still engenders argument and discussion, and is still not fully "solved".

Plato's Political Philosophy

One central concern of political philosophy is the uneasy relationship that exists between the individual and the State. The "liberal" view is that the State exists merely to serve the needs and wants of isolated free individuals. This is the view of Sophist philosophers like Thrasymachus. The "communitarian" view of Plato emphasizes the social nature of individuals. What makes us human in the first place is our group membership.

> INDIVIDUALS EXIST ONLY AS MEMBERS OF A SOCIETY. IT IS INEVITABLE THAT THEY JOIN IN SOCIETY'S ESTABLISHED SOCIAL, ECONOMIC AND POLITICAL PRACTICES.

Individuals can therefore be judged primarily in terms of their contribution to the State. And some radical communitarians like Plato stress the priority of a harmonious communal life, even if this can only be achieved at the expense of individual freedoms.

Argument by Analogy

This explains why Plato begins to clarify what "right behaviour" is by saying that just as it is easier to read big letters than small ones, so it will be easier to understand individual human beings by first looking at their societies. His analogy implies that the State is like a very large individual. Plato is fond of this kind of dubious "argument by analogy". Philosophers call it "conflation".

YOU FIRST GET SOMEONE TO AGREE WITH SOMETHING OBVIOUS ...

...BIG LETTERS ARE EASIER TO READ

... WHICH GETS THEM TO AGREE TO SOMETHING MORE DUBIOUS THAT OSTENSIBLY "FOLLOWS".

STATES HAVE PRIORITY OVER INDIVIDUALS.

How Societies Begin

Plato first has to explain how it is that individuals come to form something as complex as the State. He suggests that the first human beings lived an untroubled "natural" life and had only a few simple needs, easily satisfied. There were no problems with internal order and so no need for governments. Unfortunately, people soon developed a taste for luxuries.

THEY WILL WANT COUCHES AND TABLES AND OTHER FURNITURE, AND A VARIETY OF DELICACIES, SCENTS, PERFUMES, CALL-GIRLS AND CONFECTIONERY.

The Division of Labour

These demands can only be met by a "division of labour" or a growth in specialists whose own needs can only be provided for by more sophisticated societies. People's diets will also change. They will demand meat as well as bread and wine.

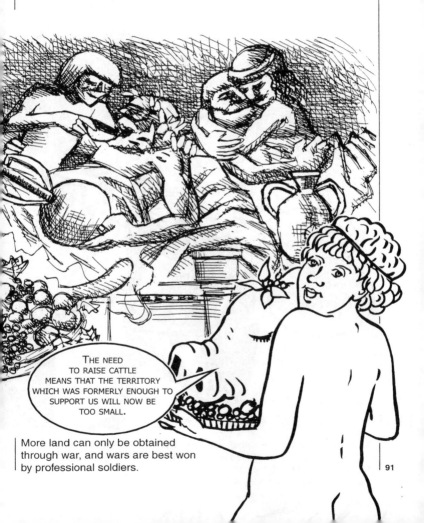

THE NEED TO RAISE CATTLE MEANS THAT THE TERRITORY WHICH WAS FORMERLY ENOUGH TO SUPPORT US WILL NOW BE TOO SMALL.

More land can only be obtained through war, and wars are best won by professional soldiers.

Educating the Republic's Soldiers

Plato was well aware of the intrinsic dangers of maintaining a professional standing army. The "guard dogs" might easily decide to become the rulers themselves. Plato's solution is to educate all soldiers in their civic responsibilities.

THE STATE MUST HAVE CONTROL OVER ALL EDUCATION.

IT CAN NO LONGER BE LEFT TO INDIVIDUAL FAMILIES OR WANDERING SOPHISTS.

Plato's own educational syllabus in *The Republic* is based on Spartan methods, which had produced an army that won wars as well as a stable and efficient society.

Athenian education was traditionally based on the study of Greek myths. Trainees for Plato's new military and administrative class would ignore the immoral stories of Greek gods.

THEY WILL STUDY ONLY MORALLY UPLIFTING TEXTS.

PHYSICAL EXERCISE AND A SIMPLE DIET FURTHER ENSURES THAT YOUNG PEOPLE WILL GROW INTO STRONG, HEALTHY AND INTELLIGENT CITIZENS.

It sounds like a rigorous and dull life. But an education like this is vitally important. If you are to give a few individuals absolute political power, then their selfless dedication to the welfare of the State is essential.

The Myth of the Four Metals

Throughout *The Republic*, Plato stresses the need for experts in every department of social life – shoemaking, medicine, seamanship and every other skill. His belief is that being a ruler is also a kind of skill, one that can be taught to a few talented and self-disciplined individuals who show an aptitude for study. These individuals will be selected from the military and promoted to the class called "Guardians".

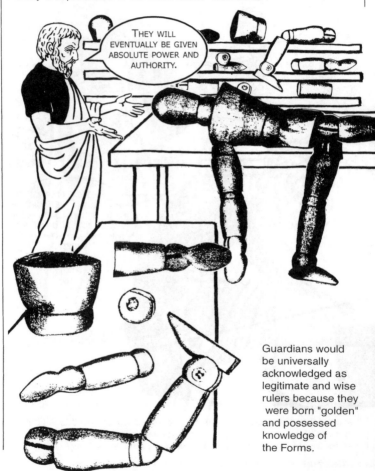

THEY WILL EVENTUALLY BE GIVEN ABSOLUTE POWER AND AUTHORITY.

Guardians would be universally acknowledged as legitimate and wise rulers because they were born "golden" and possessed knowledge of the Forms.

All citizens of the Republic must be socialized from an early age to accept this state of affairs as natural.

Everyone will be persuaded to believe the myth that all individuals are predeterminedly born as either gold, silver, iron or bronze people.

The Myth of the Cave

Plato then explains how the Guardians would be educated to know the Forms in the famous allegory of **The Prisoner and the Cave**. Once upon a time, there were prisoners kept chained in a cave from birth. Their only reality was of shadows on a wall created by objects carried in front of a fire. One prisoner manages to free himself. He turns round, and sees what is going on.

He is eventually dragged out of the dark cave into the daylight. He sees the real world, and finally the sun itself, the source of all daylight. He returns to the cave with the good news, but his fellow prisoners not only don't believe him, but threaten him with violence if he insists on repeating his adventure to them.

What Does It Mean?

Human beings are like prisoners. When they look at the material world, all they see is a misleading display of shadows and copies. A few who have "escaped" from this naive view have done so because of their knowledge of pure mathematics and geometry.

THEY KNOW THAT TRUE KNOWLEDGE COMES FROM THINKING, NOT LOOKING.

And the perfect Forms can only be "seen" mentally because they are illuminated by the primary Form of "Goodness itself" – as bright as the sun.

This is why a knowledge of mathematics is an essential preliminary to any kind of moral or political wisdom.

Their job is to enter the practical world of politics and use their special knowledge to assist the State. Therefore, because there are *two kinds* of knowledge, there must be *two kinds* of people. And one sort is destined to be ruled over by the other.

The Harmonious Beehive and the Soul

Plato's utopian Republic is hierarchical and pyramid-shaped. A few gold people (or "escaped prisoners") will be infallible Guardian-rulers. Silver people will be soldiers and civil servants. The majority are the iron and bronze folk – the producers of wealth. This harmonious beehive hums along happily because all know their place and perform their allotted tasks without question. This tripartite society is also "natural" because it parallels the construction of the individual human soul.

THE SOUL CONSISTS OF **REASON, SPIRIT** AND **APPETITE.**

These qualities are found in differing amounts in the very rational gold "Guardians", the spirited silver "auxiliaries", and the appetite-driven iron and bronze workers. A man dominated by greed is like a State ruled by the lower orders. A man who is courageous but ignorant is like a society of primitive warriors. And a perfect man and a perfect State are both ruled wisely by knowledge and reason. "Justice" (or correct behaviour) in the State is the same as justice in the individual. Plato seems convinced that if ideas seem to fall inevitably and consistently into patterns like these, then they must be true.

The Big Lie

By the second generation, everyone will believe this myth of hierarchical castes to be natural and inevitable. Plato is quite content to admit that his hierarchical society must be based on a lie.

MANY CENTURIES LATER, KARL MARX INVENTED THE TERM "IDEOLOGY" TO EXPLAIN HOW THIS LIE ACTUALLY OPERATES IN REALITY.

IDEOLOGY

ALL POLITICAL AND ECONOMIC POWER IS ALWAYS DISGUISED AS BEING "NATURAL" SO THAT IT IS MADE ACCEPTABLE.

THE MARXIST PHILOSOPHER **ANTONIO GRAMSCI** (1891-1937) WENT FURTHER.

CITIZENS ARE SOCIALIZED TO ACCEPT THIS KIND OF "HEGEMONIC" AND "NATURALIZED" POWER WHICH WILL SEEM TO THEM A PRODUCT OF THEIR OWN CONSENSUS.

Plato seems to have no moral qualms about imposing his "great lie" onto all citizens, although he omits to say whether there will be some "inner party" who will always know the lie for what it is.

The Bizarre Life of a Guardian

Plato recognized the political importance of education straight away. His "golden" Guardians indoctrinate future Guardians to ensure that the perfect Republic never changes. The lives of individual Guardians are also very controlled.

BOTH SEXES MUST LIVE IN COMMUNAL BARRACKS, OWN NO PROPERTY, AND BE RIGOROUSLY EDUCATED AS LOYAL MEMBERS OF THE STATE.

WE BREED ONLY WITH FELLOW GUARDIANS CHOSEN BY LOT.

OUR ANONYMOUS CHILDREN ARE RAISED IN STATE NURSERIES.

Plato approved of Spartan eugenics. This means that the lottery which allocates sexual partners during "breeding festivals" is always fixed to ensure that only healthy specimens get to breed. "Defective offspring" are "quietly and secretly disposed of".

Plato's Guardians are allowed no individuality or personal freedom. Their lives are regulated and monastic, communal and impersonal, dull and worthy. But they do have absolute power.

THEIR LACK OF WORLDLY POSSESSIONS AND FAMILY COMMITMENTS SHOULD MAKE THEM INCORRUPTIBLE.

HIS REPUBLIC IS MERITOCRATIC - TALENTED IRONS CAN GET PROMOTED TO GOLD.

AND IT IS NOT SEXIST.

The Guardians are an ascetic and priestly caste of political experts whose word is law. Plato clearly believed that, given time, any political and social arrangement, however odd, can eventually win acceptance and become regarded as "natural". He sees human nature as extremely malleable, so that it is quite feasible to produce female Guardians who will show no remorse when required to abandon their new-born children, and male Guardians who will never accept bribes.

The Guardians and the Forms

The absolute rule of the Guardians would be bureaucratic. There would be no "rule of law". Each particular individual citizen and situation would be judged by the Guardians against their infallible knowledge of the Forms. Democracy would be pointless, because what most people want is not necessarily what is right and true.

When the escaped prisoner finally sees the world outside the dark cave, he makes a journey from amoral darkness to the moral light of the sun, a symbol of "The Good" or "Goodness itself".

Just as we all need physical eyes to see with, so the Guardians have a special "inner eye" (or "reason") with which to "see" the Forms.

"THE GOOD" IS THE SOURCE OF ALL WISDOM, INCLUDING MORAL UNDERSTANDING.

AND IT IS THAT WHICH MAKES THE GUARDIANS INTO MORAL, AS WELL AS POLITICAL, EXPERTS.

But, by this stage, we seem to have left philosophy behind and entered the realm of political mysticism.

Moral Absolutism

Socrates maintained that morality is a special kind of knowledge which, once known, would always be chosen. Plato seems to have agreed, but argued that this knowledge must be restricted to Guardian experts who will always know the "correct" answers to all moral problems.

BECAUSE THEY CAN CONSULT THE LOFTIEST FORM – "THE GOOD" – THEY WILL BE INFALLIBLE MORAL AUTHORITIES, OBEYED BY ALL THE SILVER, BRONZE AND IRON PEOPLE.

No Place For Art

It must be emphasized that we know very little about the pre-Socratic Sophist philosophers. But some of what we do know comes from the "bad press" they got from Plato. One thing seems clear. They were defenders of art, which by its "tricks" and slippery nature calls into question the certainty of reality. Plato, we can guess, did not approve of any art, literary or visual. He asks, "What is art?" What does an artist do when he paints a flower?

HE IMITATES WHAT HE SEES — THE **COPY** OF THE IDEAL FORM OF A FLOWER.

HIS PAINTING IS A **COPY OF A COPY** AND THEREFORE **DOUBLY FALSE** …

IT IS UNCONNECTED WITH ANYTHING **REAL**.

Artists are like inspired but mendacious madmen, and are banished from Plato's utopian Republic. An officially sanctioned "State Art" would, however, be permitted.

The State of Art

Plato's conclusions on art are chilling. We can read them as grim forewarnings of what we have seen as the consequences of "state approved" art in the 20th century. Nazi doctrinaire art in Hitler's Germany, "Socialist Realism" in Stalin's Russia and the puritan horrors of the "Cultural Revolution" in Mao Tse-tung's China – are these the examples of what might happen if Plato's ideas were applied in reality?

The Paradox

And yet, by some weird paradox – or is it a basic misunderstanding? – Plato has always been a favourite philosopher of artists themselves, especially in the "neo-Platonist" version adopted by the Italian Renaissance. Plato – who condemned and banished art – became celebrated as the first real founder of aesthetics. How can this make any sense? The short answer is perhaps best provided by the neo-Platonist response of the Renaissance sculptor, painter and architect **Michelangelo Buonarroti** (1475-1564).

ART DOES NOT IMITATE A "COPY OF AN IDEAL FORM" ...

IT **SETS FREE** THE IDEAL FORM WHICH IS CONCEALED IN SILENT MATTER.

Criticisms

Plato seems to have put his faith in a "moral geometry" that would prove as certain and indisputable as mathematics. It would provide the State with total security and stability.

IT IS AN ETHICAL DOCTRINE THAT MOST MODERN PHILOSOPHERS WOULD REJECT FOR ALL SORTS OF REASONS.

IT IS ABSOLUTIST AND INFLEXIBLE.

ONCE CONSULTED, THE FORMS WILL PROVIDE MORAL PRONOUNCEMENTS THAT REMAIN PERMANENT, CLEAR, UNIVERSAL AND SO COMPULSORY FOR ALL.

But most of us now think of moral pronouncements or rules as being more like useful generalizations. It's **usually** wrong to lie and steal, but not **always** (as Socrates himself pointed out). Nor is it clear how moral codes of behaviour can ever become a branch of knowledge that can be shown to be true. What sort of evidence or demonstration could ever **prove** the truth of a moral rule like "Stealing is wrong"?

Not many philosophers now believe that there are moral "facts". Moral values are wholly different to facts, and there seems to be an "is-ought gap" lying between them. Moral codes seem more sensibly described as strongly held beliefs, feelings or universal orders. It also seems increasingly unlikely that we can "ground" human moral rules by appealing to transcendent non-human entities like the Forms. All this means that it's very unlikely that Plato's belief in moral "experts" can be justified.

SOME PEOPLE LIKE TO BE TOLD HOW TO BEHAVE IN THEIR EVERYDAY AFFAIRS.

BUT MANY THINK THAT MORALITY MUST INVOLVE SOME ELEMENT OF PERSONAL CHOICE AND COMMITMENT.

There is more to being a moral individual than just following orders issued from above. And in our own century, we are now also very suspicious of "State morality".

The Ship of State

In *The Republic*, Plato explains – in the form of two more fables – why democracy is a poor form of government. The most famous fable is the "Ship of State" story. Once upon a time, a mutinous crew took over a ship and decided to go on a pleasure cruise. They quarrelled a lot, and followed a persuasive but stupid leader.

This allegory ostensibly makes it clear why democratic systems of government are always accompanied by stupidity and disaster.

Democratic governments have to take the short-term view, and so are directionless.

It is fatal to ignore expert navigators who steer by the stars, or, of course, a government of Guardians who rule by the light of the Forms.

The Wild Beast

Plato also thought it was very easy for democratic politicians to pretend to be wise and independently-minded whilst actually being blatantly populist. They are like fake animal trainers who pretend to give commands to a wild and untrained beast.

AS THEY SEE THE ANIMAL ABOUT TO JUMP, THEY SHOUT ...

JUMP!

BUT WHO'S REALLY IN CHARGE?

Democratic politicians are merely the slaves of those they pretend to rule, and ordinary people are volatile, violent and bestial.

But fables like these aren't really proof or evidence. Society isn't a boat, rulers aren't navigators, and people aren't wild animals. A ship has a clear destination. This obviously isn't true of societies. How can we know what a society's destination should be?

A CREW AGREES TO OBEY COMMANDS FOR THE DURATION OF A VOYAGE.

BUT THE CITIZENS WHO MAKE UP SOCIETY ARE MORE LIKE BOAT-OWNERS THAN CREW-MEMBERS.

THIS IMPLIES THAT WE SHOULD HAVE A LARGE SAY IN DECIDING WHICH COURSE THE SHIP SHOULD TAKE, AND AT WHAT SPEED.

It's true that Athenian helmsmen were famous for their knowledge of the stars and their skill in navigating around the Mediterranean. But if the Forms don't exist, then it's not at all clear how the Guardians could ever "pilot" the State.

Plato and the People

Plato's political philosophy is clear enough. He believes in an absolute kind of benign dictatorship of the many by the knowledgeable few. The Guardians are the legitimate rulers because they know the Form of "The Perfect State". Ordinary people have to relinquish political rights and freedoms in exchange for harmonious order and stability.

PLATO IS THEREFORE UTTERLY HOSTILE TO ANY FORM OF DEMOCRACY. HE USUALLY ASSOCIATES IT WITH CORRUPTION AND VIOLENCE.

THE ORDINARY PEOPLE PUT SOCRATES TO DEATH, AND I NEVER FORGAVE THEM FOR IT.

Plato disliked ordinary people because they seemed to him ignorant, simple to manipulate and easily roused to mob fury.

BUT IF THEY ARE IGNORANT, THEN IT IS PROBABLY BETTER TO EDUCATE THEM THAN DESPISE THEM.

THE LIBERAL VICTORIAN PHILOSOPHER **JOHN STUART MILL** (1806-73) POINTED OUT THE EDUCATIVE MERITS OF DEMOCRACY AND FREEDOM OF SPEECH.

He argued, perhaps optimistically, that if independent individuals are allowed to argue and discuss politics, they automatically become better informed and wiser than mere obedient "subjects" ever do. And if there are hundreds of different political opinions voiced, the wisest and most practical will survive the debating process, and the silly or pernicious ideas will wither away.

117

There is no conclusive evidence from recent history to show that either Plato or Mill is right.

119

Against Utopianism

In *The Republic*, Plato says that ideals and standards are necessary if things are ever to change for the better. In *The Open Society and Its Enemies*, **Karl Popper** (1902-94) attacked Plato's political philosophy for its utopianism, which poses a danger to an "open society" of democratic freedoms.

Societies are always imperfect and evolving. They're constituted by human beings who are never perfect, and they have no clear "final destination".

Utopianists like Plato also often talk about "fresh starts" and "wiping slates clean", which implies that existing societies must be destroyed before "New Jerusalems" can be built.

REVOLUTIONARY DESTRUCTION FOR SOME REMOTE "IDEAL" USUALLY PRODUCES MISERY AND PRIVATION FOR ORDINARY PEOPLE.

PUZZLED BY THE INERTIA AND IMPERFECTION OF ORDINARY PEOPLE, UTOPIANIST VISIONARIES IMPOSE THEIR DREAM WITH AN IRON WILL.

THEY BELIEVE THEIR OPPONENTS TO BE EITHER WICKED OR STUPID!

History shows that revolutions usually engender societies that are more oppressive and unjust than the ones they replace. Plato seemed to believe that his project was so convincing that people would accept it without any protest.

What is the "Right" Government?

Before we judge Plato too harshly, we should remember that his visionary Republic has served for 2,000 years to make us *think politically* of the government that is finally best. *The Republic* ends with an analysis of different forms of government. **Timocratic** government (which valorizes property or "worth"), like that of Sparta, is obsessed with military honour.

BUT MILITARY GOVERNMENTS CAN ONLY MAINTAIN THEIR POWER BASE BY SUPPRESSING THE MAJORITY OF THE POPULATION.

OLIGARCHIES, IN WHICH THE WEALTHY RULE AND THE POOR HAVE NO SAY, INEVITABLY LEAD TO A UNIVERSAL BELIEF IN MONEY AS THE MEASURE OF EVERYTHING.

A SOCIETY OF A FEW RICH CONSUMERS WHO TREAT THE MAJORITY MERELY AS AN ECONOMIC RESOURCE IS BOTH UNJUST AND INHERENTLY UNSTABLE.

This rather suggests that Plato might have disapproved of the inequalities and excesses of present-day Western capitalism.

Democratic governments are also misguided and unstable because the mob does not possess enough intelligence or goodness to rule itself. Democracies also tolerate too many opinions – a weakness which leads to uncertainty and political chaos.

TOO MUCH LIBERTY SOON DEGENERATES INTO LAWLESSNESS.

THIS THEN LEADS TO EVEN GREATER TYRANNY.

THERE WILL ALWAYS BE SOME POTENTIAL DICTATOR WAITING TO RESTORE "LAW AND ORDER".

The absolute power then granted to some tyrant always leads to pathological excesses. If there are no laws, dictators are able to act out their darkest homicidal fantasies in reality. They become no longer rational or human, so no one is ever safe.

The Laws

It was partly this fear of despotism that made Plato recognize the importance of the rule of law. This is in spite of his earlier advocacy of dictatorial rule by the infallible "Guardians". He subsequently realized that no one should ever be above the law – especially powerful rulers. Human beings are weak and therefore vulnerable to temptations of all kinds.

Plato wrote his last book, *The Laws*, when he was old. It is a long, repetitious and often dull book. But it was his final attempt to create the template for a perfect society.

THIS TIME I AM MORE AWARE OF THE NEED FOR CHECKS AND BALANCES WHICH WILL ENSURE THAT POWER IS NEVER CONCENTRATED INTO THE HANDS OF ANY ONE INDIVIDUAL OR SMALL GROUP.

Plato's Second Republic

Plato's second Republic – his city-state of "Magnesia" – is secluded and self-sufficient. It consists of 5,040 eugenically selected land-owning citizens who are serviced by a larger population of workers (who have no political rights).

THESE SELECT CITIZENS ARE RULED BY LAWS ADMINISTERED BY 37 GUARDIANS, AND 12 SCRUTINEERS WHO ENSURE THAT THERE IS NO CORRUPTION.

The political life of the individual citizen as described in *The Laws* does seem more free and just. More people get a say in how things are run, and their freedoms are secured by the rule of law.

The Theocracy

Unfortunately, life for the individual citizen in the new and improved Republic of Magnesia isn't very appealing. Its "laws" are fixed, eternal and non-negotiable.

The State is run by the ominously-sounding "Nocturnal Council" made up of "those who know" – the interpreters of divine (and so secular) law.

Dissenters are kept in solitary confinement for up to five years, given instruction, and if that fails, eventually executed. The earlier harmonious beehive of gold, silver and iron seems almost attractive by comparison.

What Would Plato Do with Socrates?

Plato's Athenian contemporaries thought that all citizens should display outward observance to public ceremony and holy ritual, but they usually allowed individuals their own private religious views. Many of them would have disapproved of Plato's absolute and illiberal theocracy. And it's very unlikely that even five years of solitary confinement and compulsory instruction would ever have persuaded Socrates to accept such religious and political intolerance.

The Laws makes a disappointing ending to a philosophical body of work that began with a total commitment to Socrates' own freedom of speech and thought.

BECAUSE PLATO CANNOT HAVE PERFECT PEOPLE, HE INSISTS ON PERFECT LAWS WHICH MUST BE OBEYED ...

BECAUSE THEY ARE ... PERFECT.

But from the evidence of our own century, it now seems clear that dreams of perfect societies ordered by perfect laws can only be created by nightmare forms of repression.

Fortunately, not all of Plato's philosophy is exclusively about politics and power. Much of it is about other things.

The Symposium

The Symposium was probably written at about the same time as *The Republic*. "Symposia" were after-dinner drinking parties which usually involved games and entertainments of various kinds, as well as enlightened conversation. The discussion in *The Symposium* is about the "true nature of love", and is between Socrates and several famous Athenians, such as the comic playwright **Aristophanes** (c. 448–388 B.C.E.) and the political rogue **Alcibiades** (c. 450–404 B.C.E.). Aristodemus is our narrator of these conversations.

Homosexual and Heterosexual Love

The "love" they are talking about is homosexual love. For most male Athenians, heterosexual love was regarded as little more than an inferior procreative urge. Most Athenian women played very little part in public life and were confined to domestic duties. Marriage was not conceived of as a partnership between equals.

PLATO HIMSELF WAS STRONGLY ATTRACTED TO BEAUTIFUL YOUNG MEN.

AND HIS FRIENDSHIPS WITH THEM HAVE USUALLY BEEN FAIRLY DISASTROUS.

Nevertheless, he seems to have convinced himself that physical homosexual love could eventually be transformed into something transcendentally spiritual. This is why the term "platonic" has subsequently been used to describe certain kinds of non-physical relationships.

So, What Is Love?

Aristophanes, the witty playwright, has a more interesting proposition. He claims that everyone originally consisted of three genders – male, female and hermaphroditic.

As a punishment, Zeus then split everyone into single genders.

So love is always the attempt to find one's own "lost half", whether male or female.

Love is much more than a quest for sexual gratification – it is the search for a lost self.

Agathon (the host) agrees that love is a kind of yearning: it moves towards an object of beauty which remains unpossessed.

The Purer Forms

Rather surprisingly, it is a woman, Diotima, who continues the debate. She insists that love is the link between the sensible and spiritual worlds. If love is that which moves towards what is beautiful, and wisdom is beautiful, then love is the manifestation of the human soul seeking out the true wisdom of the Forms.

TRUE LOVE MUST EVENTUALLY EVOLVE INTO A PURELY SPIRITUAL QUEST WHICH EMBRACES GOODNESS AND HAPPINESS.

IT IS FOR EVER ASSOCIATED WITH THE CREATIVE FORCE THAT SUSTAINS ALL ART AND PROGRESS.

A higher and nobler kind of homosexual love leaves behind the physical world of sensation, but is not "sterile" because it "procreates" ideas and discoveries, and is one of the root causes of civilization itself.

Alcibiades Enters

Happily, it is at this point that the drunken and disreputable Alcibiades enters to bring the conversation down to a more refreshingly human level. He mocks Socrates for being so pure and self-controlled.

Everyone then eventually falls asleep or goes home.

Aristodemus (our narrator of these conversations) wakes up to see Socrates still declaiming.

The Timaeus

In this book, the chief speaker Timaeus is encouraged to provide his account of the origins of the universe. Critias then continues with the history of Athenian exploits under the guardianship of the goddess Athene at a time when the mythical city of Atlantis was defeated and destroyed.

Atlantis: Legend of the Lost City

Critias entrances everyone with his poetic evocations of Atlantis, and his descriptions of the city have subsequently hypnotized many fantasists into making dubious and unproven claims about its "real" location.

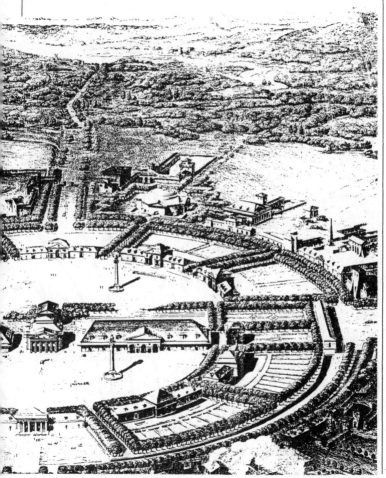

Cosmology in *The Timaeus*

Unsurprisingly, Timaeus is a spokesman of orthodox Platonism. The physical world we can see is merely the world of "becoming" – a poor copy of the "real" world of the Forms which can only ever be grasped through thought. And because this universe is imperfect, then it must have been created by some "demi-urge" or divine "labouring artist" who imposed forms onto amorphous matter.

HE MADE THE UNIVERSE SPHERICAL BECAUSE THAT IS THE MOST PERFECT AND HARMONIOUS GEOMETRICAL SHAPE.

TIME IS SIMPLY A SERIES OF NUMBERS THAT MEASURE HOW THE SUB-STANDARD COSMOS IS ALWAYS CHANGING.

Plato agrees with the pre-Socratic philosopher **Empedocles** (c. 490-430 B.C.E.) that it is the four elements of earth, air, fire and water that unite in different combinations to make up everything. There are also different sorts of living beings in the world. Human beings are the strangest of all because they possess immortal souls.

- EACH SOUL IS ASSIGNED TO A STAR TO WHICH IT RETURNS AFTER DEATH - IF ITS OWNER IS DESERVING ENOUGH.

The undeserving are unfortunately returned in recycled forms for another attempt at stellar immortality. Here it would seem that Plato subscribes to the doctrine of **metempsychosis** or reincarnation, as Pythagoras also did.

Triangular Particle-Theory

Timaeus then proceeds to explain in meticulous detail how different sorts of triangles combine in a variety of ways to make up the four different elements. As we know, Plato was convinced by the Pythagorean view of the physical universe as ultimately mathematical. He was equally aware of the reductionist theories of the pre-Socratic sceptic **Democritus** (460-370 B.C.E.).

ALL MATTER MUST IN THE END BE REDUCIBLE TO SMALL, INVISIBLE AND UNCHANGING "ATOMS" OR "UNCUTTABLES".

DEMOCRITAN ATOMS WERE IRREGULAR AND RANDOM. BUT MINE ARE PERFECT TRIANGLES.

Plato supposes that the Creator would produce a particle physics that was mathematically harmonious, and so gives us his own version – different combinations of very small triangles.

Plato and String Theory

Unfortunately, the universe isn't made up of isosceles and scalene triangles, and there seem to be about 100 elements rather than just four. So much of this speculation is now only of historical interest. But even if the specific details of Plato's physics are wrong, the underlying belief still seems sound. If human beings are ever to reach a profound understanding of the universe, then the mathematical and reductionist approach still seems the best way of getting there. We now have a fairly extensive knowledge of the infinitesimally small "things" hovering unpredictably between matter and energy that make up our universe. Much of this understanding comes from mathematics, and not just from experiments with expensive particle accelerators. Current cosmological and mathematical "thought experiments" now suggest that we live in an 11-dimensional asymmetrical universe made, not out of triangles, but of very tiny objects that vibrate like violin strings throwing off "notes" that human beings only ever perceive as energy or matter. And this wholly mathematical "M-theory" seems inherently untestable because "strings" are ridiculously small. An experimental machine to establish the theory would have to be as large as the Milky Way itself!

The Chora

The Timaeus is also full of odd and interesting ideas about what things were like before "things" themselves came into being. "Chora" is Plato's name for all the unformed matter that existed before anything was formed, categorized and labelled. So if, like many postmodernists, you believe that our experience of the world is always moderated and falsified by linguistic categories, then the concept of "Chora" is a very useful one. The semiotician and psychoanalyst **Julia Kristeva** (b. 1941) redeploys it as a term to describe all the experiences that signifiers cannot capture …

LIKE THE MYSTICAL EXPERIENCE OF THE SHARED BODILY SPACE INHABITED BY MOTHER AND CHILD.

By appropriating this Platonic concept, she can explore the nature of the often unhappy and misleading relationship that words have to human experience.

The Sophist: Puzzles and Confusions

The Sophist is Plato's major attempt to construct analytic philosophy, in which he puzzles away at the nature of "being". He examines the inadequacies of both the realist and the idealist positions. What "exists" or is "real" has to mean more than just "that which is tangible".

NO ONE DENIES THE EXISTENCE OF INTANGIBLES LIKE WISDOM, JUSTICE AND THE SOUL.

BUT WHAT IS "REAL" CAN ALSO OFTEN MOVE ABOUT AND THINK – SO THERE MUST BE MORE TO "BEING" THAN JUST IDEAS.

The Sophist is a difficult, complicated and uncertain book, mainly because of the confusions in Plato's own thoughts and language. It asks whether "being" is the same thing as "being active", and tackles many more technical philosophical problems.

Language, Thoughts and Things

The Sophist opens a hornets' nest of metaphysical confusion. The main cause of perplexity seems to lie in the verb "to be". Plato seems to think that if you say "X is hot", then you've committed yourself in some way to the belief that "X exists". This is one reason why he thought that the Forms had to have some kind of special existence.

BUT THE "IS" IN "ROBINSON IS AN ANARCHIST" ISN'T MAKING ANY CLAIMS ABOUT ROBINSON'S EXISTENCE.

IT JUST LINKS (OR "PREDICATES") HIM WITH ANARCHISM.

Nevertheless, it's an interesting book for philosophers because of the questions it raises and the linguistic puzzles it produces. Philosophers often get words, ideas and things mixed up. Some of the causes of Plato's verbal and philosophical confusions have been clarified and understood only very recently.

The Thaetetus

The Thaetetus is another technical book like *The Sophist*, in which Socrates, Thaetetus and other philosophers argue about different theories of knowledge. Plato, we know, is generally dismissive of the empirical knowledge that we derive from our senses. It is only a temporary, subjective kind of knowledge that we have about "copies". It is better than ignorance, but nothing like the "real thing". Nevertheless, in this dialogue, Plato examines how we perceive the material world and tries to explain how this perception is possible. His belief is that perception is a kind of two-way process.

THE EYE EMITS LIGHT AND THIS ENABLES IT TO PERCEIVE THE LIGHT EMITTED BY THE PARTICLES ON AN OBJECT'S SURFACE.

This explanation commits him to a theory of perception as an active process. Our senses receive "raw" data from the world, which they then convert into a form of information that we can actually use. Like many later philosophers, Plato is suggesting that our limited perception of the world and its actuality may be very different.

Sensations and Knowledge

Thaetetus, a good empiricist, argues that, in the end, human perception must be our only true source of knowledge. Socrates attacks this view by arguing that, if this were the case, then all sensory illusions, like mirages, would have to be classified as "knowledge".

> YOU WOULD ALSO BE COMMITTED TO THE ILLOGICAL BELIEF THAT EACH INDIVIDUAL SUBJECTIVE VIEW OF THE WORLD IS EQUALLY TRUE.

> IF THIS WERE THE CASE, THEN THERE COULD NEVER BE ANY RELIABLE KNOWLEDGE OF OBJECTS IN THE WORLD – JUST A SERIES OF CONFLICTING INDIVIDUAL SENSE EXPERIENCES.

Socrates is sensibly pointing out that there is more to true knowledge and understanding than just having sensory experiences. The Heraclitan world is constantly subject to motion and change. All we ever actually perceive are change-able patterns of light, shade, textures and shapes.

THIS IS WHY WE HAVE TO USE OUR MINDS TO INTERPRET WHAT WE SEE.

OUR SENSES ARE MORE LIKE COMPLEX "TOOLS" OR ABILITIES THAN SIMPLE PASSIVE RECEPTORS.

There is a great difference between "having sensations" and an "intelligent awareness".

151

Theories of Perception

In *The Thaetetus*, Plato seems at times to be moving towards some kind of "representative realist" or even "phenomenalist" theory of perception. (What we actually perceive are internal mental images of the world, rather than the external world itself.) At other times, though, he seems to be more of a naive realist. (What we perceive is indeed the world itself.)

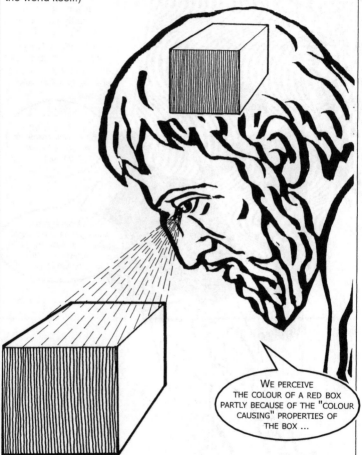

WE PERCEIVE THE COLOUR OF A RED BOX PARTLY BECAUSE OF THE "COLOUR CAUSING" PROPERTIES OF THE BOX ...

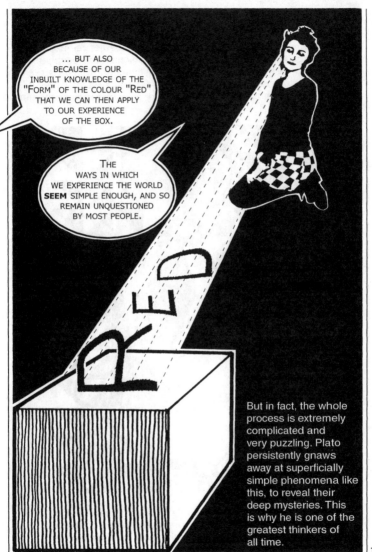

But in fact, the whole process is extremely complicated and very puzzling. Plato persistently gnaws away at superficially simple phenomena like this, to reveal their deep mysteries. This is why he is one of the greatest thinkers of all time.

How Do We Have Wrong Thoughts?

But, in the end, Plato remained a "Rationalist" – a philosopher who believes that all of the best and most permanent knowledge has to be obtained through the mind. One problem for Rationalist philosophers is: how do you know that you are having truthful thoughts? Empiricists have the luxury of being able to check their ideas against the world. If you're not sure whether penguins lay eggs or not, you can take another look.

BUT HOW DO YOU KNOW WHETHER THE WORLD IS MADE UP OF TRIANGLES OR NOT?

If you are a Rationalist, you have to rely on rather more worrying notions of mental clarity, aesthetic harmony and logical coherence. Plato worried about how it is that even the most conscientious philosophers make serious mistakes.

His answer is that false beliefs are usually caused by the vagaries of memory. Our memory is like a wax tablet, full of impressions inscribed upon it by past experiences and ideas. Sometimes we apply these memories inappropriately to present experiences, and so make mistakes.

WE THINK WE KNOW SOMEONE WE DON'T. WE ASSUME PAST THEORIES HAVE AN EXPLANATORY FORCE THEY NO LONGER POSSESS ... AND SO ON.

EVEN WORSE, SOMETIMES WE REMEMBER **ERRORS** AS TRUTHS.

The mind is like an aviary, full of colourful thoughts flying around in all directions, and sometimes we catch the wrong one. Plato isn't sure how we can ever circumvent these kinds of inbuilt cerebral defects. In the end, knowledge probably has to be that which we believe, that which is true, and that which we can clearly identify. There's more to knowledge than just having beliefs which merely "happen" to be true – knowledge has to be "tied down" in some way. But trying to define what knowledge actually is, turns out to be very hard. And all philosophers still agree about that.

The Phaedrus

This is a book about love, rhetoric and language. Phaedrus reads a speech on love by the famous orator Lysias. Socrates then extemporizes on the same subject by repeating some of the ideas found in *The Symposium*. The subsequent discussion on rhetoric, however, is more original. In *The Republic*, Plato is always scathing about the Sophists and their high estimation of "effective talk".

TRUE PHILOSOPHY IS THE COLLECTIVE SEARCH FOR WISDOM, NOT THE TEACHING OF SMART AND PERSUASIVE LINGUISTIC TRICKS TO AMBITIOUS YOUNG MEN.

BUT IN THIS DIALOGUE, SOCRATES IS GIVEN A MORE FLEXIBLE ATTITUDE.

RHETORIC IS ONLY A TOOL AND MAY BE PUT TO GOOD AS WELL AS BAD USES.

What is Rhetoric?

"Rhetoric" has come down to us today simply as high-flown, windy and empty talk. It had a completely different meaning to the Greeks. Rhetoric was a crucially important technical discovery of the way language actually works and can be manipulated. "What is it that makes language *so persuasive* to us?" Rhetoric was the investigation of this question, related to **logic** and the foundation of **semiotics** (in Greek, the "study of signs") that we still use today. These complex technicalities are examined in Aristotle's influential treatise on rhetoric. Plato was very aware of rhetorical techniques, and exploited them brilliantly in his writings.

ONE DAY YOU WILL FORGET THAT "SOPHISTICATED" DERIVES FROM "SOPHIST".

I FIGHT THE OVER-SOPHISTICATED ABUSE OF RHETORIC THAT THREATENS TO REPLACE THE SERIOUS BUSINESS OF PHILOSOPHY.

Against Writing

The dialogue ends with a thinly veiled criticism of Phaedrus for reading out someone else's ideas. Socrates condemns writing as an unnatural method of recording knowledge. Philosophy is never "complete" or "finished", but is always in the process of "becoming" which can only be maintained through live conversations and the direct action of one mind upon another.

THIS MEANS THAT TRUTH CANNOT BE FOUND IN WRITTEN TEXTS WHICH SEEM TO CLAIM COMPLETION AND FINALITY.

NOR CAN TEXTS ARGUE BACK WHEN THEY ARE MISUSED OR MISREPRESENTED.

So, concludes Socrates, the written word is useful only as an aid to memory.

Plato himself possessed a collection of scrolls, but there were no such things as libraries or "publications" in his Academy. Knowledge was always presented orally, and students were expected to argue and debate with teachers and each other. One student who did make notes on Plato's lectures lost them all at sea.

ON HIS RETURN, HE CLAIMED FINALLY TO HAVE UNDERSTOOD MY MAXIM.

ONE SHOULD WRITE, NOT IN BOOKS, BUT "IN THE SOUL".

Plato's attack on writing seems odd, given that it is a *written* argument. He was certainly no sceptic about the ability of language to reflect the nature of reality. He was, in **Jacques Derrida**'s terms, a "logocentric" philosopher. What does Derrida (b. 1930) mean by "logocentrism"?

Deconstructing Logocentrism

Logocentrism focuses on the ambiguity of the Greek word *logos*, which can refer equally to "word", "inward thought" or "reason" itself. A profound confusion begins here.

> PLATO GIVES SPEECH PRIORITY OVER WRITING BECAUSE HE PRESUMES THERE IS SOMETHING "OUTSIDE THE TEXT" THAT GIVES IT A FIXED MEANING.

> THIS IS WHAT I MEAN BY BEING "LOGOS-CENTRED".

Western philosophy since Plato has mistakenly assumed that language somehow mirrors the "correct meaning" of objective reality. Derrida's criticism or **deconstruction** of philosophical texts exposes their hidden metaphorical nature and unconscious beliefs, of which the writer remains unaware. For instance, in *The Phaedrus*, Plato can maintain that the written word is both a "poison" and a "cure" by deploying the term *pharmakon*, which has these multiple senses of medicine, remedy, poison, drug, charm, enchantment, and so on. Derrida shows that Plato's own language often works directly against the ideas it intends to convey.

Private and Public Voices

But although *The Phaedrus* text may itself be teased into revealing some internal inconsistencies, its central critique remains. Until very recently, most of the words human beings heard were spoken to them as individuals by someone standing nearby. But now we live in the world of mass media. Language in our postmodern world seems far removed from any individual speaker. We access all kinds of "information", but often have no way of knowing its origins or intentions. The World Wide Web floats ideas made of algorithmic pixels into cyberspace – all of which can be manipulated in a hundred ways.

INTERNET DISCOURSE IS PRODUCED BY THOSE WHOSE IDENTITIES ARE OFTEN FICTIONAL OR HIDDEN. SO, PLATO HAS A POINT.

DIRECT DISCUSSION WITH KNOWN INDIVIDUALS IN A SUNLIT ATHENIAN GROVE DOES SEEM PREFERABLE.

Plato's Inheritors: Aristotle

Aristotle listened to Plato for nearly 20 years and was one of his more argumentative students. He disagreed with many of Plato's ideas. In his *Metaphysics*, he criticized the Platonic Forms for being impossibly transcendent and mystical. He sensibly maintained that Forms and particulars don't exist separately.

FORMS ARE INCORPORATED IN INDIVIDUAL PARTICULARS AS POTENTIALITY.

OR, PUT MORE SIMPLY: ALL PARTICULAR ACORNS POSSESS THE FORM OF THE POTENTIAL OAK TREE.

By close examination of particulars in nature, it is possible to draw inductive conclusions about how the world works and what powerful forces control it – the methodology that is at the heart of empirical science.

Aristotle's ethics also seem more reasonable. Morality isn't some special kind of knowledge like mathematics that only a few can attain.

IT'S AN ATTITUDE OF MIND AND A PRACTICAL WAY OF BEHAVING THAT ANYONE CAN ACHIEVE IF THEY'RE GIVEN ENOUGH TRAINING AND EXPERIENCE.

But although Aristotle's philosophy is very different from Plato's, he always praised his teacher for asking the right questions. Plato got philosophy started as an academic discipline.

Platonists, Neo-Platonists and Others

Plato's Academy survived for nearly 1,000 years, until it was finally closed down by the Christian Emperor Justinian in A.D. 529. Neo-Platonists like the early Christian Church Father Origen and Plotinus converted many Platonic ideas of goodness, the soul and immortality into sophisticated theology. Aristotle had greater influence than Plato on medieval scholastic thought. Plato's texts were preserved and commentated on by Islamic scholars like Avicenna, and thanks to them his "rediscovery" in the Italian Renaissance influenced Petrarch, Erasmus, Thomas More and other scholars to question the dogmas of scholasticism. Galileo, the first "modern" physicist, admired *The Timaeus*, which reinforced his own anti-Aristotelian view.

(1) Velocity $\cdot \dfrac{distance}{time}$, or: $\dfrac{V}{2} - \dfrac{S}{t}$

n the figure it is evident that: $V \cdot gt$

$: \dfrac{gt}{2} \cdot \dfrac{S}{t}$

Falling Bodi

NATURE MUST HAVE AN UNDERLYING MATHEMATICAL STRUCTURE.

Increasing velocity

$g \cdot$ acceleration

Average velocity $\bar{x}$

Each period in European philosophy reclaims its own "Plato".

And we have seen how Plato stimulates postmodernists like Jacques Derrida and Julia Kristeva. It looks like Plato's ideas will survive for a very long time yet.

What Sort of Philosopher Is He?

The pre-Socratics survive only in sparse enigmatic fragments. So, if Socrates, a talker not a writer, appears as the world's first *recognizable* philosopher, this is entirely thanks to Plato's written reports of what he said. Plato is also a more systematic thinker who put his own ideas into writing. He produced nearly all of the central questions for philosophy in epistemology, metaphysics, ethics, politics and aesthetics.

AND I WROTE ON MUCH ELSE BESIDES, FROM EDUCATION TO BEEKEEPING.

Many of the questions that Plato raises are quite practical.

> WHAT SORTS OF LAWS DO WE NEED IN ORDER TO PRODUCE A JUST SOCIETY?

Others are more metaphysical and technical.

> WHAT IS "REALITY"? WHAT ARE UNIVERSALS?

Often they stimulate the activity that modern philosophers now call "conceptual analysis".

> WHAT IS "JUSTICE"?

This tends to make philosophy more of a "second order" discipline – you criticize what other people say and analyse the language they employ to put their case.

What Does a Philosopher Do?

5th-century B.C.E. Athens certainly was a very talkative town, full of different views of human nature, society and the role of philosophy, with plenty of cynicism about all three. And some sceptical Sophist views about the limitations of human knowledge now seem very "postmodern". Plato's critical reaction to them was to discover what the philosopher's task really is.

IT IS, FIRST, TO EXAMINE THE SORTS OF QUESTIONS THAT ARE BEING ASKED.

AND SECOND, TO ANALYSE THE HUGE VARIETY OF ANSWERS THEY PRODUCE.

It's all too easy to ask impossible questions and then be content with nonsensical or superficial answers. This may explain why most of Plato's work is in dialogue form – because it investigates and interrogates.

Dialogue Interrogation

Time after time, Plato's Socrates asks an important question and various individuals of very differing abilities make stabs at producing answers, often in the form of inconclusive and unsatisfactory definitions.

THESE ARE THEN ARGUED OVER AND REFUTED ...

AND REPLACED BY YET MORE HYPOTHESES ...

... WHICH ARE THEMSELVES TESTED.

AN EXHAUSTIVE PROCESS WHICH ENDS ONLY BECAUSE EVERYONE REACHES AN AGREEMENT THAT IT IS TIME TO GO HOME TO BED.

For those who are not used to philosophy, this can make reading Plato a frustrating experience. This is especially true if they believe, damn it, that it is the philosopher's job to give us all some clear and conclusive answers to the crucial and often worrying questions that always seem to arise out of human experience.

What Are the Answers?

Plato would have had some sympathy with this more challenging job description. He didn't think that philosophy was just a matter of detached logical analysis. Philosophy was an extremely serious moral business. He thought he could provide answers to many of these questions. He believed that the world was ordered rationally. Mathematics had therefore to be the key to understanding how it all worked.

ENCODED IN THE UNIVERSE AND THE HUMAN MIND ARE CERTAIN UNALTERABLE ETERNAL TRUTHS ABOUT MATHEMATICS, MORALITY AND POLITICS.

A FEW EXPERTS COULD REDISCOVER THESE TRUTHS BY DEVELOPING SPECIAL VISIONARY POWERS.

THEY GET TO "SEE" A GHOSTLY "PYRAMID" OF FORMS TOPPED OFF BY THE GLOWING MAJESTY OF "THE GOOD".

This semi-religious experience made them infallible, legitimized their moral authority and gave them absolute political power.

The Quest for Ideal Perfection

These mystical doctrines are usually presented to us dogmatically as articles of faith, or explained in parable form with allegories of prisoners and caves, ships and crews. Plato's powerful prose style often creates the impression that his philosophy is coherent and clear. But surprisingly, the central doctrines of "Platonism" are neither lucid nor argued with much logical rigour.

PLATO HAD AN IMAGINATIVE LONGING FOR A PURER, MORE RELIABLE WORLD THAN THE SHABBY AND INADEQUATE ONE THAT HE WAS STUCK WITH.

He is also guilty of persuading too many philosophers to think that philosophy is a quest for secret arcane knowledge restricted to a few self-appointed specialists. His political philosophy is productive, because we always need ideals. But it can also be very destructive. It now seems that utopianist dreams cannot be actualized without totalitarian methods.

171

Plato, the Escape-Artist

It is difficult to pin Plato down. He seems to be not one philosopher but several: a tentative clarifier of conceptual confusions; a dogmatic élitist who advocated a ruthless dictatorship based on eugenicist principles; an inventor of better worlds. A neo-Platonist called Olympiodorus said that Plato once dreamt he was a swan, flying from tree to tree, in an attempt to escape some huntsmen's arrows.

The Greeks took their dreams very seriously. Olympiodorus interpreted this dream to mean that the real Plato would always escape from all commentators and interpreters. His philosophy could never be tied down to one single doctrine. For Plato, philosophy was always the beginning, and not the end, of inquiry. With that we can only agree, and use it as a good excuse to finish this book.

Further Reading

Plato's works are nearly all available as Penguin Classics or in other paperback editions. Plato's early accounts of Socrates' life and teachings, and his most famous work, *The Republic*, are all accessible and entertaining, unlike much modern philosophical writing. Plato's philosophical writings are difficult to date precisely, partly because there were no such things as "publication dates". No one is very certain of the order of their composition. It seems very probable that they were all written in the 4th century, after the death of Socrates in 399 B.C.E., and that *The Republic* was written circa 375 B.C.E. The works are usually divided into early, middle and late periods. *The Apology*, *Crito*, *Euthyphro*, *Laches*, *Charmides*, *Meno*, *Protagoras*, *Cratylus* and *Gorgias* are presumed to be early. *The Symposium*, *Republic* and *Phaedrus* are middle. *The Parmenides*, *Thaetetus*, *Sophist*, *Timaeus*, *Critias* and *Laws* are thought to be late works, although there are still disputes about the dating of works like *The Timaeus* and *Cratylus*.

Books on the civilization and philosophy of ancient Greece.

The Greeks, H.D.F. Kitto (Penguin, London 1951). This is still one of the clearest and most accessible guides to ancient Greece and its inhabitants.

The Cambridge Companion to Early Greek Philosophy, ed. A.A. Long (Cambridge University Press, 1999) is a collection of several very useful essays on different pre-Socratics.

A History of Greek Philosophy, W.K.C. Guthrie (Cambridge University Press, 1979) is for the real enthusiast. It comes in five volumes and covers everyone from Thales to Plato.

Other useful introductory books.

Early Greek Philosophy, Jonathan Barnes (Penguin, London 1987).

An Introduction to Greek Philosophy, J.V. Luce (Thames and Hudson, London 1992).

For light relief, the reader can turn to *The History of Greek Philosophy* by Luciano de Crescenzo (Picador, London 1989), wherein can be found an account of the philosophical views of the pre-Socratics, the Sophists, and some Neapolitan acquaintances of the author.

There are lots of books on Plato. Here are a few.

Plato, R.M. Hare (Past Masters Series, Oxford University Press, 1982). This is an excellent, if occasionally quite difficult, short introduction to the complexities of Plato's philosophical ideas.

Understanding Plato, David J. Melling (Oxford University Press, 1987) is short, clear and accessible.

An Examination of Plato's Doctrines, I.M. Crombie (Routledge, London 1963). This comes in two volumes, is extremely thorough and comprehensive, and is probably for more experienced readers of philosophy.

Plato's Republic: A Philosophical Commentary, R.C. Cross and A.D. Woozley (Macmillan, London 1964). A book for those who wish to read *The Republic* and think about all of the philosophical issues it raises in more detail.

The Cambridge Companion to Plato (Cambridge University Press, 1993) is a collection of 14 useful essays on different aspects of Plato's philosophy.

This writer also enjoyed reading I.F. Stone's hatchet job on Socrates, *The Trial of Socrates* (Picador, London 1989) and *Love's Knowledge* by Martha C. Nussbaum (Oxford University Press, 1990).

The Open Society and Its Enemies (Vol. 1), Karl Popper (Routledge, London 1966) is still the most influential critical analysis of Plato's political philosophy.

Acknowledgements
The author would like to thank all of the students with whom he has studied Plato's philosophy. They helped him identify and clarify problems and even provided him with a few answers. So Socrates' firm views about philosophy as an activity may be right after all. He would also like to thank Judy Groves for her artistic imagination and friendship, and the patient and painstaking work of his long-suffering editor Richard Appignanesi who, amongst many other things, knows how to use the comma and the semi-colon.

The artist would like to thank Oscar Zarate who contributed some excellent drawings, Arabella Anderson and Deane Waerea for allowing me to photograph them for this book, and David King and Howard Peters for their help with picture research.

Index